MAN AND WOMAN
GOD MADE THEM

Also by Jean Vanier

Community and Growth
From Brokenness to Community
Becoming Human
Seeing Beyond Depression
Drawn into the Mystery of Jesus through the Gospel of John
Encountering "the Other"

Related Titles

Prayer of Heart and Body
The Miracle, the Message, the Story

MAN AND WOMAN GOD MADE THEM

JEAN VANIER

PAULIST PRESS
New York/Mahwah, N.J.

I want to thank very particularly George Durner, Kurt Armstrong, Martha Bala and Jock Dalrymple for having helped me rework the original text in order to bring further precision and clarity.

This edition published in 2008 by
Paulist Press
997 Macarthur Boulevard
Mahwah, New Jersey 07430

Originally published in French by Editions Fleurus and Editions Bellarmin in
1984 under the title *Homme et Femme Il Les Fit*
Copyright © 1984, Editions Fleurus, Paris
Copyright © 1984, Editions Bellarmin, Montreal
English translation © 1985, 2008, Darton, Longman and Todd

This edition published by arrangement with
Darton, Longman and Todd Ltd
1 Spencer Court
140-142 Wandsworth High Street
London SW18 4JJ

ISBN 978-0-8091-4555-3

Library of Congress Control Number: 2007935739

Designed by Sandie Boccacci
Phototypeset in 11/14pt Bembo
Printed and bound in Great Britain

Contents

INTRODUCTION

The first edition of this book was written twenty-five years ago, at a time when people with a learning disability were, in a certain sense, coming out of hiding. Throughout the centuries in our Western society, they had most often remained hidden in their families or behind the walls of institutions. People tended to believe that they were, at best, like children or, at worst, were in some way 'sub human', an 'error of nature'.

These ideas still exist in many places in our world today. There has been, however, a constantly growing movement towards welcoming people with a learning disability into our society and our churches. Many are being helped to develop the skills necessary for independent living and working. They are being opened up to the world. The progress is excellent. Increasingly, society is recognising that people with learning disabilities are above all *persons*; they have the right to find their place and to live as full a life as possible.

There is a danger though that in the process of finding their place in society, they will also experience rejection, loneliness and isolation if not properly accompanied and assisted. In many instances, once they have their job and a place to live, they are expected to be 'just like everybody else' in the sense that they need to 'make it on their own', just like everyone else. But they are not like everyone else. People can forget that in some ways they are different. Their physical and intellectual difficulties can be a real source of anxiety or fear in people who do not know them. This makes it difficult for people with a learning disability to meet others. They are not invited over for a cup of coffee like other new neighbours. To really take their place in society they need help and support, especially to meet others and to make friends. Like all of us they have vulnerable hearts, but do not have the same defence mechanisms and capacities to make choices as others. They can be easily rejected, hurt and manipulated.

Over these last twenty-five years, the media and internet have developed a great number of films and DVDs which portray sexuality in a superficial and sometimes pornographic way. Sexuality has not been portrayed as a gift that grows out of a permanent relationship and strengthens and deepens that relationship. People with a learning disability can be confused by these films. They can be seduced into sexual relationships without an awareness of the consequences or the capacity to assume responsibility for a partner.

After coming out of 'hiding', and now finding themselves in mixed residences and workshops, or in outside employment, they can be attracted to all forms of sexual relationships and easily seduced and abused. From being considered 'like children' to becoming 'like any other adult', they can be put into complex and confusing situations. I believe that more than ever that people with a learning disability need to find places of belonging and community, where on the one hand there is the support that is needed as well as a feeling of friendship and togetherness, and on the other where they have a place of privacy and the freedom to grow humanly and spiritually.

Although in richer countries much progress has been made in helping people with a learning disability to have access to education, housing and work, much still has to be done. Parents who discover during pregnancy that their child has a severe disability will seek an abortion. For many to have a child with a disability is too great a burden. People with a learning disability are still put aside; they have few friends and are not well accepted and integrated into the local area. Many people are still frightened of them.

Man and Woman God Made Them is about the importance of relationships and community as the place where people with a learning disability can grow and develop both humanly and spiritually, where they can grow in a faithful love. Community is a school of love. Relationships, however, are never easy. Each one of us has been hurt more or less during our early childhood and so we in turn have a tendency to hurt other people. Relationships need to be deepened and transformed so that they can be celebrated in fidelity.

This book was written from a Christian perspective because I believe, as St Paul tells us, that God has chosen the weak and the 'foolish' according to the world in order to confound the strong and so-called wise (cf. 1 Corinthians 1). Since they live close to the heart, people with learning disabilities can be open to the message of Jesus which is essentially a message for the heart. That is why the message of Jesus gives ultimate meaning of the lives of people with disabilities.

Readers might find the order of the chapters a bit strange. When I began living with men and women with a learning disability, I discovered quickly their brokenness: hearts crying out for healing and for an authentic love. So, that is how I began this book, writing one chapter at a time as I lived it. The book ends in a song of celebration, together in community, where each one has grown in inner freedom and maturity.

This book is about relationships between men and women. I have chosen not to go into questions around people with a homosexual orientation. We all share the same humanity. We are all brothers and sisters in front of God, but the questions concerning homosexual orientation are different and need to be respected in their difference. Many suffer immensely today from discrimination; their pain and anger are understandable. Integration of sexuality into a mature relationship is a long and sometimes difficult journey for all of us.

Finally a word about language: I use the politically correct phrase 'people with a learning disability'. Different expressions can be used in different countries. What is essential is that people with learning disabilities are people. They are important human beings who must be allowed and helped to grow to greater fulfilment with all their abilities as well as their disabilities.

Chapter One

THE WOUNDED HEART

The Disillusionment of Parents

So many couples hope and yearn for a baby, to give life to another human being, a person who is like a seal on their union. The immense joy for a woman of being pregnant. The dream of having a beautiful baby boy or girl. The preparations: choosing a name, preparing the bedroom with a cot, the baby clothes ... The body of the mother begins to change and at one moment she feels the little one beginning to move within her. Then one day the couple is told that the baby may be disabled. The shock! Their disbelief: it is not possible; it must be a mistake. Then later the doctor tells them, sometimes quite brutally: 'Your child has a severe disability. We can do nothing. Put the baby away and plan to have another as soon as possible.' In an instant, their hearts are crushed, their hopes shattered; and grief rises up and the questions: 'Why has this happened to us? What have we done to deserve this?' Then, because it is necessary to blame someone, comes the terrible question: 'Whose fault is this?' In the Gospel (John 9:2) the apostles ask the question about the man born blind: 'Master, who has sinned, this man or his parents?' They are asking: 'Who is guilty?' Is the child with a disability a punishment from God? And if so, how can the fault be expiated?

I am touched more and more by the pain and difficulties of parents. We in l'Arche have our days off, our holidays, our times of renewal and spiritual refreshment. We have chosen to live with such vulnerable people. Parents have no days off, little support and no chance to refresh their spirits. They did not choose their child to be 'like that'. For them, it is a tragedy, a personal humiliation, and constant suffering. We in l'Arche are often admired for our 'dedication'; parents, on the other hand, are often pitied or looked down upon. A whole school of thought even blames them, especially if the child is psychotic. Many heroic parents live long days and often nights with terribly disturbed children. Sometimes there are no schools, centres or special workshops near their homes. They do not have competent or understanding psychologists and doctors to encourage and support them. Often shunned or pitied by neighbours, friends, and even family and church, they find themselves utterly alone. Some believe they have been punished by God and they close in on themselves in isolation and anguish.

The Suffering of the Child

All these sufferings deeply affect the child. It is a terrible thing for children to feel that they have let their parents down and are the cause of their pain and their tears. The wounded hearts of parents wound the heart of the child. Children can sense whether or not they are a source of joy, the centre of delighted attention, one whom everyone wants to touch, to hug and to hold. They sense their parent's pride and joy as each new skill is gradually developed and acquired. Between the baby and the parents, there is a life-giving dialogue which stimulates, calls forth, encourages and supports. Even the tiniest babies sense whether or not they are truly precious for their parents, loved by them in a unique way. Children with a severe disability can sense that they are a cause of pain.

Sometimes I am asked: 'Is a child or an adult who has a severe intellectual disability aware of his or her condition? Do they suffer from this?' For the most part, I don't know. But this I do know: the tiniest of infants sense whether or not they are loved and wanted. Similarly, persons with disabilities, even severe ones, sense immediately whether or not they are loved and valued by the tone of the voice and by the way they are touched and looked at and welcomed.

Newborn children are extremely fragile and vulnerable. Unable to do anything alone, they need to be fed, washed and held. There is only one recourse, which is to cry. If the baby feels responded to, loved and valued, there is a feeling of security and safety; the baby is able to live, to be at ease and, to enter with confidence into relationships with others and with the reality of the world. However, when infants do not feel responded to, loved and valued, they have a sense of being in danger; people and the surroundings become threatening. They enter into the world of fear and insecurity, where they instinctively harden themselves for protection and survival. Isolated in their inner world, they suffer terribly and live in anguish.

Children can also live in anguish and experience a form of interior pain if their mother is too possessive and has invested herself too exclusively in them. Somehow she communicates that the only safe and loving place in the world is with her, instilling a fear of separation and smothering life. All children sooner or later are called to leave their parents. Therefore, they must learn early in life to cope with separation and frustration. This is as necessary for their growth as it is to be loved and valued. True love does not imprison; it liberates. A mother cannot be occupied totally with her child; she has a husband also, and she has her own needs. Children must learn the frustrations and longings of separation in order to discover the joys of reunion with parents and to put their confidence in the bonds which unite them all together.

Few people seem to understand the depth of the anguish of a tiny child who is not loved or who is 'badly' loved. Fortunately, scientific research, focusing on the newborn infant, is discovering today what mothers have always known: that the relationship between the mother and child is profoundly sacred and precious, a source of life for them both. The same is true, of course, for the father, but in a different manner.

Today, human science has ascertained, in part, that a newborn infant can not only see and hear (though in a very limited way), but can even recognise the smell of its mother. We know that an intense dialogue, harmony, relationship already exist between the baby and the mother – even before the child is born. If that relationship is defective, if the little one does not sense its mother's love – which not only rejoices in her baby's beauty and uniqueness, but also in its potential for growth, for autonomy and eventual separation from her – then the baby feels lost and enters into anguish. It experiences either an inner emptiness or an inner suffocation.

Anguish

Anguish is a terrible reality, one of the greatest of human sufferings. This is why it is used in torture. When victims of torture suffer total anguish, there is a sense of terrible confusion, of being utterly lost. Their inner will is completely broken and eventually they can be unable to keep any secret.

Anguish first reveals itself in the region of the solar plexus, the physical seat of the emotions, and then spreads throughout the whole body. Inner balance is broken, and the person becomes agitated, confused, unable to reason or to judge. The normal digestive and sleep cycles are destroyed, with a tendency to eat and sleep too much or not at all.

This state of anguish is so painful that it cannot be tolerated for long. In order to survive and escape the pain, children protect themselves by creating defences and hiding in a world of dreams. There is a cutting off from the heart because the heart searches continuously for contact with love, and not finding it, this constant, unfulfilled desire to be loved becomes unbearable. When the heart of a person is solidly barricaded in this way, there is a form of psychosis. If the barriers are less solid, there can be instability, sometimes depression, agitation, apathy or aggression.

In the case of adolescents or adults, the defences may take on different forms. Some escape into hyperactivity, a desire to succeed, to win, to dominate in school, in sports, in work, etc.; others search for compensation in alcohol, drugs, sexual encounters and a continual search for distraction and pleasure. Still others can sink into deep depression, mental illnesses or delinquency.

When I see Evelyn banging her head against the floor, when I hear Robert in the middle of the night begging someone to cut off his genitals, when I see Luke aimlessly running round and round, when I see the closed, tense face of George, I know in each there is a profound agony and an unbearable interior restlessness.

Little children who have learning disabilities and who know they are not wanted will harden their hearts and body to protect themselves and to withdraw from reality. They live a sort of inner death: life no longer evolves. Agitation can prevent development. Certain aspects of the psychic being can become blocked. The brain, language and even physical development can be affected. Thus begins the fragmentation of their being.

I remember Mark seated next to me in the chapel, whispering over and over: 'I have the devil in me. I have evil in me.' His story is a story of rejection. Born in a psychiatric hospital, abandoned by his mother, he was adopted, but this did not work out. He then went from one foster family to another. After a time, he was placed in a small institution and then sent to a psychiatric hospital because he had shown signs of violence. At the age of twenty-seven, he came to l'Arche. Never in his life had he had a lasting and unique relationship with an adult. Having been moved from one place to another as a child, he had never heard anyone say to him, 'You are my beloved son and you are my joy. Between us is an indestructible bond. No matter what you do, you will always be my child.' Mark was without any roots.

If one has never been loved, how can one believe oneself to be lovable? And if one is not lovable, then it must be because one is no good. The logic of love is relentless. Because no one ever had confidence in him, because no one had ever formed a bond with him, Mark was unable to have confidence in himself. He had a negative image of himself. Perhaps he is an extreme example, but many people with disabilities suffer from the image they have been given of themselves. The way we look at others has a profound effect on their self-image. There is always a message transmitted with our eyes: it can be approval, affection, indifference, scorn, distaste, etc. When we constantly avoid looking at certain persons, they immediately sense rejection or repulsion. Over time they will have the feeling of being worthless, even to themselves. Eventually, they too will avoid looking at themselves. This is often the story for those excluded from our society because of a disability or others reasons.

Carol was welcomed into one of our communities. She had been considered a crazy idiot since her early childhood and is imprisoned in that image and continually tries to live up to it.

I remember Michael who, when he won a gold medal in the Special Olympics, wept and cried out: 'Do you think that now my mother will believe I am good for something?'

There was Gertrude who, when asked if she would like to be married some day, replied: 'I will never marry because my mother told me that if I married I might have a child like me.'

I am always struck by the way each is the reflection of how he or she is seen by others. Gloria, who lives in a l'Arche community in a Latin-American slum, acts so differently now compared to the time when she was with her family who scorned her. At home, family and neighbours looked on her as the 'village idiot'. In our home, where she is treated with hope, respect and understanding, she is adjusting more and more; her personality is becoming more structured despite her crises. Girls like her lie in wait to see if others look at them in fear, judgement, scorn, and superiority, or with understanding, kindness and joy in her presence. The eyes of another reveal to us who we are. 'Who am I for you?' Gloria is so much who we see her to be. And she is capable of interpreting the tiniest nuance: 'You love me because I gave you a gift? You love me because I am making progress? You love me because through me you found a meaning to your life?' Or, rather, 'You love me for me, because my life means something?'

These are only a few examples. I could give hundreds of others, showing the deep pain of people with intellectual disabilities and how the negative, broken image they have of themselves comes from the image others have of them. Dr Dolto, a child psychiatrist, at a session for special educators in France, once explained how the psychotic child identifies him/herself with human excrement. Always feeling rejection, always perceiving themselves as bad, identifying themselves with what is rejected as waste and smells bad.

I am always impressed by the love people with intellectual disabilities have for their parents, even when they may have been mistreated and abandoned. They always hope for the happy and loving reunion with their parents, even when their waiting and their hope are so often disappointed and dashed to the ground. I have never heard one of them criticise or judge his or her parents. The tragedy is that as a coping mechanism, they may condemn themselves as if they deserved their parents' rejection. They feel and develop a profound sense of guilt because they feel it is they who are bad. To be rejected by the parent, the trusted adults in whom the child relies for sustenance, shelter and meaning, is profoundly destabilising. The child's whole world falls apart. It is better then for the child to believe that 'I deserve this rejection', giving him/her some pittance of control over the emotional chagrin. 'If I accept the fault, then I can also hold onto the hope that by trying harder things may improve.' This hope is obviously doomed to fail and reinforces the agony and isolation of rejection.

Let me tell you about Betty. She had lived with an impossible mother. She had endured so much that now she is unable to live with any woman assistant without persecuting her, without avenging herself. But, is it truly revenge? Is it not rather a cry: 'You see, you will never be able to love me; I am too bad.' Thus, she relives the conflict with her mother.

One of the difficulties of the child, which can also be found between engaged couples or husband and wife, is to idealise the parent (or the other) and to turn them into idols. They become like gods who ought to fulfil every need. When this doesn't happen, then the child either feels it is their own fault or else they reject the one who has not lived up to expectations. It is so difficult in any relationship to accept the loved one as a fallible person who also has needs, and to avoid projecting one's own needs on to the other.

I remember a meeting at l'Arche to discuss a man who had been severely rejected by his family and who was quite disturbed. Dr Franko, the psychiatrist of our community at that time, said of him: 'He feels guilty for existing.' So many of the men and women we welcome into l'Arche have been considered to be difficult and unbearable by their families (and often they have been). They have been treated only in negative terms, as 'deficient', 'handicapped'. It is not surprising they feel guilty, responsible for the tears and anguish of their parents. It is not surprising that they have cut themselves off from their hearts; they have suffered too much. They cannot bear the pain any more.

This deep wound of the heart is the source of their bizarre behaviour, whether aggressive or depressive. Not having been recognised as true human beings, capable of growth, they can have difficulty forming a true relationship with another. Some have always been considered by others as an object and so will consider others as objects; they cannot imagine that they are capable of giving life and happiness to another. In order to live they must make the transition from a negative self-image to a positive image, from a feeling of being without value to a feeling of being valued. Who will help them make this transition?

This inner fragmentation is not restricted to people who have an intellectual disability. It can be found in all hurt and unwanted children, children who feel they are a burden. These, too, must protect themselves from unbearable pain. I remember a prisoner, condemned for kidnapping a child, telling me that his mother had told him when he was eight years old: 'If the contraceptives had worked, you would not be here today.'

Symptoms of depression are often found, not only in such children, but also in people who are scorned because of their race, their poverty, or their inabilities.

It becomes clearer and clearer to me each day, however, that these same wounds are found, though to a lesser degree, in the hearts of *all* children. Every child, at one time or another, has felt more or less let down by their parents, unloved, unappreciated and even rejected Parents go through periods of depression; they are taken up by their own problems and needs and do not give adequate attention to caring for their child. The heart of a child is so vulnerable and sensitive! Often these wounds remain in the unconscious, producing difficulties in future relationships and even in the use of one's sexuality.

Most children have the inner strength and outer competencies to react to feelings of rejection; they have the strength and ability to separate themselves from their parents. Persons with disabilities, on the other hand, who may have certain strengths or other outward competences, may feel very lost in the face of rejection and tend to withdraw into a form of 'non life' or profound despair. Their barriers are less developed than in other children whose defence mechanisms are more solid, strengthened by their inner power. That is why many with disabilities let down their barriers more quickly when they are offered an authentic relationship.

It seems evident, however, to anyone who is in contact with different kinds of families, united or divided, with whatever kind of parents, over-protective or unloving or very present and loving – that a wounded heart is not produced in a child only by their parents' attitudes. Even the most marvellous parents can never fulfil every hope and need in the child. They are able to love their child, but they are not able to ensure that the child's heart will itself be loving. Certainly, in children, there is great innocence and beauty but, regardless of all the qualities of their parents, there are also all kinds of fear, fragility and egotism. In the heart of every child there is a void which can be filled only by an infinite love. This is the glory and the tragedy of humankind. St Augustine's words, 'My heart is restless until it rests in God', apply to each and every human being. The wounded heart of every child, with its fears and selfishness, comes from an awareness – more or less conscious – of this emptiness deep within our being which we desperately try to fill, but which we find nothing can totally satisfy. This void is a source of inner anguish but, if the child has even a minimum of confidence, this anguish can become a driving force towards a search for commitment to others and truth.

Christian doctrine on the wounded heart, or original sin, appears to me the one reality which is easily verified. It would be an error to believe that if there were no oppressive parents, if there was no oppressive society, then we would have only beautiful, loving, happy children integrated within themselves. No, in the heart of each of us there are divisions, fears and fragility; there is a defence system which protects our vulnerability, there is flight from pain and there is darkness. However, children who live in a loving relationship which helps and truly gives them support, will find hope and trust more easily to go forward in the search for true fulfilment.

Healing the Heart

Eric was sixteen years old when we welcomed him to l'Arche some years ago. He had been placed in a hospital at the age of four; he was blind, deaf, severely brain-damaged and his heart terribly wounded by being abandoned by his family.

In the hospital there were doctors and nurses who cared for him, but none were able to answer the deep cries of his heart. They were not there to establish lasting and loving relationships with him. Hospitals are not homes but places for treatment.

The body of a child who senses he/she is loved is secure and relaxed. A child who feels abandoned and alone becomes rigid and tense, so as not to suffer too much anguish. Thus it was with Eric, deaf and blind, who protected himself against an environment which he perceived as hostile, because it was incapable of responding to his cry and his enormous need for tenderness. The rigidity of Eric's heart was reflected in the rigidity of his whole body. His muscles were like wood. When he came to us, he could not walk.

Eric would only re-find his desire to live when he could discover that he was loved by another person and that there were real and lasting bonds between them – not possessive bonds, but bonds which could liberate.

Since Eric was deaf and blind, this relationship could only be established through a touch filled with tenderness and respect, a touch which reassured him and showed him that he was supported and loved, that he was safe. It was important to spend a lot of time with Eric's body, bathing him, feeding him, walking and playing with him. Only through the constant fidelity of this touch could he gradually gain confidence and discover that he was lovable and able to grow, that he was valued. During the seven years he was at l'Arche, Eric became more peaceful. No longer did he try, in a crazy way, to climb up every adult in his thirst to be touched. However, he still remained disturbed; there were still doors firmly locked within him, and his body remained rigid. We did not find the key which would allow him to completely open his heart and reveal his vulnerability and his capacity to respond with con- fidence to love. Perhaps that would have put him in too much danger. For to open his heart would have been to relive certain agonies and traumas of his early childhood, and particularly the experience of being abandoned; it would have meant accepting the risk of a new failure in a relationship, a new abandonment. Would he ever have been able to take such a risk? We cannot know. After about seven years in l'Arche he seemed to lose some of the peace he had found and some months later he died.

In another l'Arche community, we welcomed Yvette from a psychiatric centre. She was ten years old then and had suffered repeated rejection. She had always been called 'the mad child'. She hid the reality of her heart behind many aggressive and anti-social gestures. It took a long time for the leader of the community to meet her behind all those barriers. On arriving, Yvette was not ready to give her trust at the first overture. Those who have been terribly wounded, as she was, will not open up easily; they are suspicious of kind words, of kind people. Yvette did not want to live through another experience of desertion, so it was better not to create new relationships; she hid and closed herself up. Then, Yvette began to test the love shown her by making mischief and by running away: 'Are you really concerned about me?' 'Do you really love me?' Then came the day when the innocent child within her dared to believe that she was loved. Yvette accepted the tenderness; she opened the door of her heart. However, very quickly she shut it again. But, for an instant, for the first time, she had tasted the joy of communion with another person. Some days later, she dared to open herself up again to tenderness: she then began a game of hide and seek, a going and coming, until the day when she was able almost totally to open her heart. She had found peace. She had accepted dialogue. She had found trust in an adult. Today, she knows she is loved and appreciated; is 'at home'; she is learning to love others and serve those weaker than herself. But it took much time and attention, much suffering and many battles before she was able to make the transition. During the dark days, the community leader, speaking of Yvette, said to me: 'In order for her to come out of herself and live, our hope in her must be deeper than the despair within her.'

Eric and Yvette needed a healing love. It was not simply a question of loving a child who had a disability, but of loving a wounded child who had lost all confidence in self and in others, who was broken and entrenched behind barriers. Such children need a love which will put them together again and lead them to wholeness. Some children are so wounded that they are obliged to cut themselves off from their hearts and the pain of the past. They have built inner barriers in order to forget those agonising times. However, in order to have a future, to have hope, it is often necessary that we come to terms with our past. The discovery of peace and liberation, and the possibility of growth, depend on the integration of our being which includes the integration of the past. Some people are never able to do this; their wounds are too severe.

A healing love permits children or adolescents, or even adults, to live through essential aspects of parental love which were denied to them. They need to discover a deep and lasting bond with an adult. They need to experience the joy that an adult has in being with them and to discover that an adult has confidence in them, is proud of them and of their growth. This love must be very concrete and bring them back to a relationship with their own bodies.

Through this love made of tenderness, forgiveness and respect these young people can begin to discover the beauty and even sacredness of their own bodies. As they begin to be at ease with their own body, to consider it as precious, they can then perhaps approach a true relationship with the body of another person.

This inner healing and liberation takes time and despite all efforts, it may never come about fully. The adolescent young man with or without disabilities can remain divided in himself and disturbed and unable to find the right boundaries to relationships; or else he seeks too quickly a close physical relationship, which is dangerous for him and for the other person because sooner or later it leads to rejection; or else he hides behind walls which have been built over the years and flees from all relationships. So it is that separation can be accentuated between genital sexuality and the heart, between the search for sexual pleasure for self and the search for a deep, authentic relationship with another. In the face of this suffering, the most important thing we can do is to accept and continue living with the person, respecting the wound in them, but keeping hope for them alive in our hearts. All of us carry wounds that will never be healed, which mean that relationships remain complicated and difficult for all of us, especially physical, sexual relationships. We are never really healed, really liberated.

What motivates us to continue to struggle to maintain our relationships to continue efforts to be more and more sensitive and tender with those we love and to be increasingly open and respectful to those persons who try our patience to the very end?

The Role of the Intermediary

In order to open oneself to others and to the world, a wounded person needs to find someone who acts as an intermediary. When a true relationship is established, the barriers slowly begin to fall, the person is able to leave the prison of sorrow and fear in which he or she was enclosed. Discovering confidence in oneself, it is no longer necessary to fight others and one's surroundings in the same way. Little by little one can begin to trust them too. Little by little, the capacity to listen, to welcome and to experience wonder grows, and one can open oneself to others and to the universe in trust. The intermediary is like a rock upon which a person can lean, a source to which one can return to be sustained, confirmed and encouraged. Unfortunately many people never find the intermediary in whom they can trust completely.

In the world of education, intermediaries play a major role. They replace the parents when these have been lacking, those parents who should have been the first intermediaries; protecting, supporting, and awakening the heart and spirit of their child. The intermediary must approach the child gently, in order to create a relationship of trust. The child needs to sense that he or she is loved and respected by someone who wishes to live a covenant relationship, not wanting to manipulate, crush or impose, but wanting only the liberation and growth of the child. Before suggesting solutions, however good they may be, the intermediary must first discover the beauty of the wounded person, hidden under the fears, the depression and the violence. In effect, to love is not primarily *to do* something for someone, but it is *to reveal* to that person his or her value, not only through listening and tenderness, through love and kindness, but also through a certain competence and faithful commitment. Our challenge in l'Arche is to find and form those who will be such intermediaries, who are called to work with others in a team, just as husband and wife are called to be the first educators together. It is all the more important to work together and be supported by professionals when it is a question of helping someone who has been deeply wounded.

The Experience of God's Love

Children who have an experience of God early in life, will grow more peacefully and truthfully. This is even more true for children or adults who have known rejection because of their intellectual disability. Those who are able to discover, either directly or through the love of intermediaries, that they are children of the Father, will be able more readily to drop those barriers which have been built around their vulnerable hearts, and they will experience a certain wholeness. To live an experience of being forgiven, washed in the living waters which spring forth from the heart of God, can, little by little, erase the feelings of guilt which are often so tenacious. Some can flee the harshness and dangers of the world by entering into a spiritual world detached from reality.

When a child has lived through unbearable pain and has been obliged to withdraw behind thick walls, this meeting with God may appear less simple and clear. It may even seem that the walls around the heart prevent the meeting with Jesus. However, there are signs, tiny signs, which occasionally may be perceived, showing that Jesus is there, hidden behind the walls. He is the only hope in all these sufferings of the heart. Children can grow, however, and have to face conflicts and seductions of the world; they can lose their childlikeness and become casualties in the struggle for survival.

The message of Jesus is truly good news. It is not, first of all, a series of laws which we must obey. It is an experience of a loving encounter with Jesus, in faith and tenderness. This encounter, which opens us to the universe and to the Father, reveals that we are precious in the eyes of God. The negative image we have of ourselves will gradually begin to lose its power over us. When we discover we are loved by the Father, we can begin to trust our-selves more; our hearts are on the road to being healed even though we remain burdened with many untransformed weak-nesses and limits. This experience gives hope. The call of God is within us like a seed; with other people we can grow in the Church, in the community of those who believe in Jesus and who wish to serve him in the way of the Beatitudes. Growth, however, always implies struggle.

One of the great sources of pain for children with learning disabilities is that the thirst to be loved is so exacting that parents are not able to respond adequately. All of us are wounded in our hearts; all of us have been wounded by our own parents and by life. We all have difficulties with relationships, and barriers behind which we hide. Parents love their children, but they have their own fears. They, too, have been wounded by their own parents and by life. Sometimes they are unable to love and accept their child with gentleness and tenderness. Their hidden aggressiveness can manifest itself unjustly. This is why it is indispensable that parents learn to speak about moments when they have been unjust and to ask for forgiveness. It is important to be vigilant in choosing the appropriate time for the child to discover their parents' limits, a time when it will not result in insecurity for the child. If children identify their parents as the source of everything, as God, they make their parents into idols that are worshipped rather than icons which signify the presence of God. They can then be unable to accept that not everything in their parents is good. When they discover later on that their parents are not God, they can become angry with them and reject them violently. If, however, parents introduce their children to the mystery of God, their children will discover that parents are not alone and all powerful; they are not the prime source of life; they can have their faults. The parents are then able to ask forgiveness of their children when they make mistakes. The children and parents are together before God as brothers and sisters, praying and asking forgiveness together.

When children or adolescents discover through their experience of a Christian community that it is possible to have a personal relationship with God, they can live their relationship with their parents in a new, more peaceful way, no longer blaming them when their expectations are disappointed. Even if they are sometimes disappointed, it is still possible to love their parents. In discovering the fidelity and compassion of God, through Jesus who is the Good Shepherd who loves and forgives, who truly leads and supports each one, and who always remains faithful, it becomes easier to drop one's barriers. This love of God lived in the community of the Church is not a figment of the imagination, springing from a disillusioned and broken heart; it is truly an inner experience.

Not long ago, Donald, who has an intellectual disability, said to me: 'During Father Gilbert's homily, my heart was burning.' Many people with disabilities, and many children, can have this experience of a burning heart. Unfortunately many 'adults' don't believe in these inner experiences of those with learning disabilities.

When the children discover an absolute in relationship with God, it is possible to accept relativity in human relationships, especially with their parents. Children can discover that interpersonal relations are neither ideal nor impossible. They are a reality which exists, but with difficulty, with many failures, reverses, hurts, but also a reality full of joy which is deepened through a thousand pardons and reconciliations. In this reality, the ambivalent and conditional relationship with its message, 'If you are good, I love you; if you are bad, I reject you', is transcended.

When a child experiences a relationship with God, he or she can discover faithfulness, pardon, and the reality of a covenant relationship. Because of the covenant with God, covenant with parents and others becomes possible. Relationship is no longer based on compatibility, but on a covenant. Then the bonds between people are more profound than emotions, feelings and even capacities for love and hate. There, forgiveness is possible.

When there is a relationship with God it is easier for the child to live the relationship with their parents as a covenant. Likewise, in all the 'ups and downs' of life, it is easier for a man to live a permanent and deep relationship with a woman, and for a woman with a man, if they have both discovered that neither one will ever be able totally to fulfil the other. They are not God for one another. They both have their wounds, interior flaws, sins and infidelities; both are called to grow to greater wholeness. In order to live and deepen the covenant between them, to mutually accept the differences and limitations, they need to have confidence in the absolute of a relationship with Jesus.

A little boy with a learning disability made his first communion in a parish in Paris. After the Eucharist there was a family gathering. The boy's uncle, who was also his godfather, said to the mother: 'Wasn't the liturgy beautiful! The only thing that is sad is that he didn't understand anything.' The little boy heard his uncle, and with tears in his eyes told his mother: 'Don't worry

Mummy, Jesus loves me as I am.' Yes, God has chosen the weak and the so-called foolish of this world in order to confound the strong and so-called wise!

Loss, Grief and the Love of God

Human life generally begins with a period of acquisition: in childhood and youth, one acquires knowledge, friendships, all sorts of goods. Then, at a certain moment, even as a child but also as an adult, we begin to live a series of losses because change implies loss. Adolescents lose their childhood. Then they lose their adolescence. Then people have health problems, loss of work, loss of friends, until there comes the final loss, of life. These losses mark painful passages in a person's history which can sometimes be shattering. They are followed by a period of bereavement during which one enters, more or less, into the cycle of depression–aggression. But, after this time of grieving, positive strengths spring up again, allowing the person to accept the new situation and to move forward on the road of life in a new and creative way.

The particular drama of those with disabilities is that these losses often come too early in life, before they have acquired the inner strength that would enable them to face loss. Sometimes loss comes at birth, or even during the pregnancy, when the baby is deprived of the love and esteem of their parents, affecting physical and psychic development. These losses, and the grief which follows, invade the child's life prematurely, when he or she has neither the strength nor the human means to cope. Moreover, sometimes children have to face such profound distress that it can be overcome only if someone becomes deeply committed to them and helps them to discover that they are loved by God, that through it all they are precious to God just as they are, in their very being. That love of God gives meaning to life, it gives strength to continue living; it enables the person to break out of the cycle of sorrow and anger; it stops the flight into illusion. This can imply that if the child does not overcome this profound distress, there is no deep inward experience of the love of God. I do not believe that is true. God is there. His love is there and there needs to be no connection with whether or not the child overcomes her profound distress. The love of God, deeply felt and experienced, mysteriously does not exempt us from pain and anguish

I remember a mother who had lost her six-year-old son. She told me that when her son was three-and-a-half-years old, he had been struck down by a paralysis of his legs which gradually invaded his whole body, and he became blind. Some months before he died, his mother was weeping at his side. Her little one said to her: 'Don't cry, Mummy. I still have a heart to love my Mummy.' That small boy had attained a real maturity; he knew how to give thanks for what he had, rather than weep for what he had not. Such maturity often comes from an inner experience of God which, I believe, is given to people who are particularly wounded and who, because of their weaknesses, would not otherwise be able to continue living. In order to receive this experience, however, the person in distress needs to be in supportive surroundings.

I met a woman who had known a lot of brokenness in her life. One day, while she was sitting under a tree, she lived a deep experience of God. She told me: 'This experience in one sense changed nothing in my life. Yet at the same time it changed everything.' The presence of God transforms us even if we are still left in the midst of our human frailness.

Chapter Two

EDUCATION AND ITS
DEMANDS

The Child's Need for a United Environment

Growth towards fullness of the heart and inner unity implies not only loving relationships but also the presence of a loving and unified family life.

The child is the fruit of a man and a woman, and ideally, the fruit of an act of tenderness and of love. During the years of development, the child needs the relationship with both a man and a woman. Unity and harmony between the man and woman are necessary for the child's healthy emotional development. If they are divided, the child will experience division within and can easily enter into a state of confusion. The child who senses conflict between the parents can live in a state of insecurity similar to that of the abandoned or inadequately loved child. In this insecurity, the child learns to protect the heart by building barriers, creating an appearance of hardness, self-sufficiency and freedom. It is intolerable for a child who loves both parents to feel one parent rejecting the other, forcing the child in some way to choose between them. A natural consequence may be a vacillation between the two according to the situation, which can quickly become a game in which conflicts and the demands of education and growth are avoided.

Certain deviations and sexual difficulties in a child can arise from the lack of unity between their parents. The body of man is made to be united with the body of woman. The psychology of one is complementary to the psychology of the other. They are created to be companions and friends; they are made to have children and to educate them together. The gifts of one harmonise with the gifts of the other; their differences are enriching. If, at the dawn of life, the child senses discord, rivalry and even hatred between them, then the development of the child, sexual or otherwise, will suffer. There can rise up in the child later a fear of the opposite sex; differences between the sexes may be seen as sources of conflict rather than as a potential for harmony.

When parents are living in continual discord, the mother or the father tends to depend too much on one of their children because they feel forsaken by the other. Only when the man finds a refuge and support in his wife, and the woman in her husband, are they freed not only to love their child, but to educate and help him or her to grow.

The emotional life of the child whose father is totally absent cannot develop in a healthy way. The mother tends to seek in her child the fulfilment of her own emotional needs, because she feels abandoned by her husband and experiences an inner void; if she takes on the attitude of 'spouse' with her son or companion with her daughter instead of mother and educator, she risks warping the normal development of the child's sexuality and personality. The mother fears losing her child. She fears the eventual separation, in which, having already been abandoned by her husband, she will find herself utterly alone. Consciously or unconsciously, she can try to prevent her son from becoming attached to any other woman. She can create in him a fear of separation from her, and a fear of other women, whose presence will engender anguish, obscurely reminding him of how his mother impeded his liberty and his desire to grow. He can then be blocked in his relations with women, and can possibly never be able to live a unique relationship in marriage. In a similar way the mother can try to prevent her daughter from leaving her for another man by constantly criticising the father and telling the daughter that men cannot be trusted. A comparable situation in the case of a father with his daughter will similarly affect her ability to relate to another man.

In families where there is only one adult and a child living together, the relationship risks becoming unhealthy for both. Healing the heart and moving toward personal wholeness is much more difficult through a relationship limited to two people. The adult risks becoming too attached to the child, or not attached enough; and the child will become either too dependent or aggressive. If the attachment becomes, as it often does, too possessive, the adult, in satisfying his or her own emotional needs, is afraid of anything that could lead to separation. As a result, the freedom to educate, to be firm with the child, is lost. This means that when a husband and wife are divorced or separated, it is important that they dialogue together about their children's education. If this is not possible, it is important that a third person be introduced into the relationship, a friend, an uncle or an aunt.

All that has been said in regard to the healthy development of children is even more vital for a child who has an intellectual disability. When there is inner division, there is a tendency to project it on the outer situation. Such a child can exploit the parents' flaws and weaknesses in order to manipulate them and to satisfy his or her own instincts, avoiding the efforts necessary for real growth. For the integration of one's being, one needs to be surrounded by men and women who co-operate harmoniously.

Without this unity in their environment the adolescent or adult with disabilities will have more difficulty in assuming the demands of growth and healing. A wound in the body heals naturally if the body is healthy. But the heart cannot heal itself. It needs to be surrounded by others who can call the person out of the fears that paralyse the heart and into a world of trust and openness with others. In order to find an inner harmony and to be at ease with his masculinity, the adolescent or the man with a disability will need the presence of men who are at ease with their own masculinity – this means those who are able to have simple, open, true and unifying relationships with women without dominating them or being dominated by them, who are able to recognise in women their gifts and qualities which are different from their own. The same, of course, holds true for women in order to be able to discover their femininity.

The 'Yes' to Growth

Gloria, of whom we spoke earlier, is now forty years old. Her disability is slight. Before coming to us, she had been dragged into the world of prostitution. Emotionally she is terribly disturbed. Little by little, she became attached to the assistants of our community. Finding a certain stability, she began to be happy there. But, there was still a pull in her to her former life. The house leader said to me one day: 'Now, Gloria must choose. She must choose life or death, either to root herself here or to return to her former life; we are not able to make the choice for her.'

It is impossible to break down another person's inner barricade. Certainly, the love, goodness and firmness of adults who confirm and give security are indispensable, but the person must open up freely, even if he or she has a severe disability. Here we touch the secret place of each one's personal freedom. Some people are attached to their blockages and their prisons; they prefer the familiar to the unknown. It seems easier to remain in the slavery of sadness and of depression, than dare to advance in insecurity along the road to liberation. Some pleasures, like drugs, briefly give a feeling of life, of well-being. Momentarily anguish is taken away. It is difficult to free oneself from these seductive pleasures which lead not to life, but to death.

To live with deeply wounded people solidly barricaded behind their iron bars is a real challenge! But we must not give up. We must continue to struggle against the iron bars that imprison the person, with ever more patience and dialogue, ever more prayer. This requires truthfulness, fidelity and the competence of professionals. It demands an ever deeper commitment. We cannot fight the battle alone. In order to help a person say 'yes' to growth we need to work together as a team, deeply united.

Tenderness Is Not Enough

The starting point of human growth is in acceptance and love. The child's first home is in the womb of the mother, then it is in the arms of the mother and father. This is both a place of rest and a space where life blossoms and develops. In an atmosphere of love and protection, the child feels secure. All education is based on that welcome and the mutual confidence it engenders. Indeed, a child will make efforts only if he or she feels loved and respected, not treated as an object or as unimportant. If the child is seen as a person with whom one speaks respectfully as to another human being, the child can then be confident, knowing that someone trusts him or her.

Demands made on children without appreciation and understanding of their inner being will provoke reactions. Feelings of anger and rebellion can rise up, even if they cannot be expressed openly. Adults will be seen as those who crush liberty and the fullness of one's desires. Law will appear stifling and dangerous. This happens when parents abuse their authority, and seek to control their children out of their own need and to satisfy their own pride, instead of freeing their children's gifts.

In the Gospel of John, Jesus speaks of the good shepherd who knows each of his sheep by name. This implies that he has listened to each one attentively. Jesus distinguishes between the good shepherd and the hired worker who runs away when he sees the wolf coming. The good shepherd gives his life for his sheep. The sheep have confidence in him because they sense that he truly loves them and really wants them to live fully, that he is even ready to sacrifice his own personal interests for them.

A child who has no confidence in authority will have great difficulty accepting the demands it makes. Confidence will be lost when there is ambiguity or a dichotomy between words and actions. A son is unable to accept the demands of a father who makes no demands on himself, or who does not love and recognise the son as a person in his own right.

I remember a young man whom I interviewed for a television programme. He had lived in the world of drugs. I asked him to speak of his experiences. Then, I asked him what his parents thought of it all. 'They were furious,' he told me. 'And what was your reaction to that?' I asked. This young man, sixteen years old, looked me straight in the eyes and answered angrily: 'Sir, my father is an alcoholic.' This young man sensed a double message coming from his father which made him lose trust in his father. If his father had said to him: 'My son, don't be like me. I know what it is like to be a prisoner of an addiction. Don't make yourself unhappy as I am,' the son would have understood and, perhaps, he could have accepted. That would not be a double message, but truth: truth demanded that the father be honest and humble.

For children to grow and to acquire a true inner dignity, it is not sufficient to be loved with tenderness and accepted as they are. They equally have a need to be encouraged, strengthened and guided by a parent or a substitute parent, true and good educators who believe in them and their capacity for growth. The parent, or the substitute parent, must prove to them that that they are truly loved and that he or she is really interested in their well-being and development. Children who sense that their father or mother is more interested in his or her own reputation, work or leisure, or that their child's presence is a nuisance, will tend not to heed their parent's advice or guidance. Walls are built between the child and authority.

The Challenge of Education

In a sense, all education involves a struggle. The growth of a child or of an adolescent is exacting: it requires an effort. It is easier for a mother to wash her son if he has a disability than to teach him to wash himself. Education demands time and patience, especially when the child lacks self-confidence or an easy capacity to learn.

It is not easy constantly to call forth a person with a disability. It is not easy to find the right balance between listening and challenging to growth, or between letting the child be and constraint.

The goal of all education is liberation. This implies both a liberation from those instincts which enslave and impede living in truth and reality, and liberation to develop the gifts and the qualities of the person to the full.

However, these two forms of liberation can be realised only if the person has space to live and to grow. We are all like plants, requiring sufficient room to put down our roots. Plants need water, air and sun. Children need to be loved, to be supported and affirmed. They need an environment which will encourage their growth and efforts, but they also need adults who will help them in the struggle against the powers of darkness and the refusal to live.

In 1981, I went to live at La Forestière, one of our homes for ten men and women with severe mental disabilities. I was astonished the first time I saw Evelyn throw herself out of her wheelchair. At that time she was nineteen-years-old; since then she has died. She had a severe developmental disability: she could not speak and had little control of her body. Only one of her arms worked reasonably well. When I stooped down to help her get back into her chair, Maria, the assistant who was with her, stopped me. Maria then, with a severe tone in her voice angrily told Evelyn not to act up like this and to get back into her chair. A struggle began between the two of them. Evelyn waited to see what was going to happen; but seeing that Maria was not going to give in, she gradually began to crawl towards her chair and to try to get in it again. That took a great deal of effort on her part. It was only then that Maria helped her get back into her chair. For many people with severe disabilities, it can be much easier to let others do everything for them than to try to do some things by themselves.

It is always up to the individual to freely say 'yes' to growth and to making the necessary efforts that this implies.

The Courage to Forbid

We live in a society where many are afraid of the demands of true education. There is a tendency to say that one must be tolerant and allow each person to fulfil freely their own needs, to follow their own ideas and instincts. Many have difficulty in exercising authority with love, firmness and wisdom. They are frightened of oppressive authority, perhaps because they had an authoritarian upbringing and so they were not helped to assume true responsibility.

Education implies that one knows when and how to forbid. There will be a time to forbid alcohol to someone who is in danger of becoming an alcoholic. It may be necessary to forbid a man with disabilities to cycle in the village if there is a real danger he will hit someone or cause an accident. Similarly, it is right to discourage a woman with disabilities from going out alone if there is danger that she may be molested. We have to prevent anyone from striking or exploiting a weaker person. There are times when we must do everything we can to prevent someone from closing up in an inner world of depression or fantasy. We need to bring the person back to where the source of life and beauty can be discovered. All this takes time, love and firmness.

If a relationship between a man and woman with disabilities seems restricted only to 'sex' without any real friendship, or if the relationship is not fostering the growth of either but, on the contrary, is leading them to new forms of enslavement or brokenness and preventing them from becoming more human, then we must have the courage to help them discover that they are on the road to brokenness and that they should stop. To allow them to continue such a relationship would be to show a lack of respect towards each of them, and a lack of hope in their capacity to live in true freedom.

Sometimes, however, it is necessary to give people the space to discover the lessons of life for themselves and even to touch the depths of their misery. For some, it is only through the experience of real failure that a dialogue can be initiated and growth can begin. It is not possible to grow to greater love if there is no space for error. In the parable of the prodigal son in the gospel of Luke, the father let his son go away, knowing that he would probably do foolish things. All of us have so many illusions. Some think that they know everything; others that there is no danger, or that they will be able to extricate themselves from any danger on their own – they refuse to listen to someone more experienced. Sometimes it is necessary for such people to experience failure.

But, this way of learning is not always practical for those with a learning disabilities, especially in the areas of alcohol, drugs, violence and the exercise of sexuality. We cannot allow them to destroy themselves or to destroy others. The risks must always be carefully weighed.

Freud talks a lot about taboos. In his time a century ago a religion of fear was preached. If one disobeyed the law, one was rejected by the community or one risked (so it was taught) being condemned to hell. This can lead to a form of neurosis. However the religion of Jesus is a religion of mercy. Jesus came not for the just, but for sinners. He desires life, not death. Prohibition for a Christian is not the same as taboo. It is not final, and fear is not the prime motivation. Forgiveness and love transcend the fear. To prohibit is to help someone move towards true liberation. It is only one element of education. But if we forbid something without a positive orientation toward some other alternative activity or without any dialogue, we may just crush the person. If they have neither the strength nor the motivation to conform to the prohibition, the attraction to the easy way out, to pleasure, to compensations or to the need to assert oneself is too strong.

Education of the Heart

Many people with learning disabilities come to us without having received any real education. They have been trained at a psychiatric hospital or centre where they were obliged to conform to its laws through fear of punishment or the promise of privileges. This is not true education; it is, rather, the way animals are trained.

Life in community requires the recognition of certain rules, the acceptance and respect of others. If we want to be the centre of attention, to have always the biggest piece of cake, then we will live in a state of continual conflict. We will tend then to crush those who are weaker, to search for companions who agree with us, to avoid all those who seem to oppose us. It is a struggle in which all seek their own interests and, in those interests, manipulate others. A human being who does not think of others and their needs sows the seeds of division and conflict.

Similarly, our society and our world are divided, with walls of fear raised between individuals, groups and nations. The poor are crushed while more and more armaments pile up for defence or attack. Nations cannot live harmoniously together if each is focused only on its own self-interest.

This individualistic attitude is the negation of love. It leads to sexual activity, and other behaviours concerned only with selfish pleasure. It does not engage the heart in a true and harmonious relationship which expresses a real communion with and tenderness for the other, confirming and helping the other towards fulfilment.

The fundamental principle of all education is to open the heart and the mind to the needs of others. This implies a certain quality of observation and of listening. There is an education of the intelligence through concepts and knowledge. There is also an education of both the heart and the will in love and service to others.

The essence of education is to lead a person into relationships with others, in openness and sensitivity to their limitations and in response to their needs. Maturity is growth in responsibility for oneself and for others.

In the fourteenth and fifteenth centuries it was debated whether or not slaves had souls and if they had a real inner life and were capable of making choices. Today, some people doubt whether people with severe learning disabilities are capable of an inner life and of love. Some want to introduce such people to sexual pleasure as a right, without helping them to discover the joy of loving and being in communion with another person.

The aim of education at l'Arche is to help each one to welcome people just as they are, to appreciate them, to see their beauty, and to respond to their needs for true growth and liberation.

Certainly it is important for everyone to grow in autonomy. But it is more important to develop one's capacities, not as an end in itself, but in order to better enter into communication with others and to build with them – not against them – a world of justice where each one feels responsible for others. People with disabilities are capable of such love. And in fact they are perhaps more able to relate to others more deeply than those who are caught up in the search for wealth, in knowledge, power and possessions.

People with intellectual disabilities tend to live closer to their hearts. Their perception and awareness are more emotional and affectionate than rational. On the other hand, people who have developed their reasoning capacities often have more difficulty relating with others freely. They live on the level of logic and competition, wanting to prove that they are the best. Intellectual faculties, powers of reason, and the capacity for action are often used to prove their superiority and to dominate others. Or else they fall into a seeking friendship for their own pleasure or usefulness.

I do not believe that the capacity to give freely and lovingly comes only after a long development of the rational faculties. Certain theories of child development give the impression that the child is fundamentally selfish, only able to receive and consume. It is implied that until a more advanced stage of intellectual de-velopment has been reached, children are unable to discover that they are part of a greater whole. It is implied that gift of self is purely rational and willed. My experience with those adults whose reason and will are less developed gives no evidence they are unable to love freely and unselfishly, or that their hearts remain on the level of subjective feelings, incapable of union with another.

A newborn child lives in a profound communion with their mother. The baby both receives life and gives life. Children love and want to express this love. They need their mother and the security she gives, but beyond this, they live a unique experience of a relationship with her. Children may not be rationally conscious of that love, but they sense the peace engendered by it. The child who is loved as a unique person experiences a sense of well-being and the revelation of his or her own beauty; the child is aware of receiving life and strength from the mother. The baby expresses love through the gift of a joyful smile and quiet trust. The child, in communion with the mother, gives to her without reserve, without fear, confident of being loved. This in turn gives life to the mother, reveals to her her own beauty and the truth of her fruitfulness, her capacity to give life, not only biologically but spiritually, through love and communion.

As children grow and develop, their innocence, the joys of communion and their wonder in the discovery of the world are tarnished. In their vulnerability, their immense emotional needs and almost infinite thirst to be loved, children can easily be wounded by their parents' lack of attention, whether deliberate or, more often, unconscious. Parents can give their unconditional love to children when they are babies. After the first months, however, parents often tend to get too busy with life, and of course with the other children. This lack of unconditional attention can open a wound in children's hearts, which is that original flaw of which we spoke earlier. A series of barriers are then created because the feelings of inner emptiness, pain and anguish – coming from a feeling of rejection – are unbearable. Yet, these barriers and even parental limitations will have a positive side; they oblige children to begin to separate themselves from their parents and to work through frustrations. These wounds become harmful when the children's fragility, because of their disability, makes it too hard to bear these frustrations or to overcome the anguish. Then, they may flounder in a sea of sadness. Alternatively, if the pain is too great and too early in life, the response will be an attempt to cut off the pain and, in so doing, to cut off the deep feelings of the heart. Defences are built up and may become more or less impenetrable.

When their hearts have been hurt, healthy children tend to turn toward knowledge, power and personal success in different domains in order to forge their identity and find self esteem. As they no longer feel unique in terms of love and communion, children will seek to prove themselves and to be unique in terms of action and production, or with friends. They may find it difficult to direct their gifts of intelligence and activity towards the service of others. Children will tend to act in order to prove themselves, to be admired by the peer group, to dominate, and to have a feeling of superiority, in order to compensate for a sense of inferiority.

In the gospels, when Jesus tells us that we must become like little children, he reveals that which is most profound and divine in a human being. Behind all the barriers built up since childhood, there is the pure and innocent heart of a child where the gift of God resides. This heart is capable of receiving and giving love, of living in communion with another person and with God, capable of being a source of life for others. But as soon as their heart is wounded, children can close up in themselves. In the design of God, it is the heart which is meant to inspire all human activities. A special grace or gift of God is necessary in order to keep the wounded heart open.

The great suffering and initial sin of human beings is no longer to believe in the innocence of communion and mutual trust which open us up to others, to the whole world and to God. It is to let ourselves be seduced by efficiency, power, freedom, pleasure and material possessions rather than building one's life on love and welcome, with all the risks of suffering that entails. It is to close oneself up upon oneself.

Sartre, in his book *Being and Nothingness,* sees love only as a battle where one person wins and decides and the other loses and becomes dependent. He seems to ignore the reality of communion, which is different from 'fusion', which implies the disappearance of one or the other, or both. Communion is a union 'with' the other which respects, deepens and strengthens the identity of each one; but, this communion is only possible if we have had a true experience of freely offered love, where the other does not wish 'to eat us up' and make us dependent – a love which, on the contrary, helps us to grow and discover who we are and what is best in us.

So often people hide behind masks – personal barriers of knowledge, power and wealth – fearful of relationships and dialogue, sometimes suspicious of love. Love can appear to them as no more than a manipulation or a desire to possess the other, preventing that person from being him or herself. Dependence seems to be a loss of freedom, a form of death. So, they harden themselves against this possibility and, in so doing, they hurt others.

Love and People with Learning Disabilities

In some ways, the masks adopted by those with an intellectual disability are often less permanent precisely because they are less rational. Certainly, when they feel too alone and abandoned, they will react like everyone else. There will be a need to affirm themselves by dominating and winning, or else they can fall into a cycle of sadness, depression and anger, or want to prove that they exist through opposition and rebellion, crying out constantly: 'No, I won't!' However, if there is the discovery of being loved and believed in, that part of the heart which is most pure and innocent, and which searches for communion and celebration, will rise more quickly to the surface of consciousness. Such persons are able to enter more quickly into communion with others, to love them in a spirit of self-giving.

Helping persons with disabilities to discover the source of life within them needs someone who will call forth and awaken their innate, hidden powers of love and communion. Often, people see only their limitations, their deficiency, rather than the gift they can bring to the human community. Who can believe that communion, compassion and welcome are human values when society around us tends to testify to the contrary? In a world where in order to be someone you have to be strong, win, and conform to the values portrayed in the mass media, persons with learning disabilities will always remain at the bottom of society's ladder, despite all the efforts of normalisation. It is not surprising then that many of them remain sad and depressed, struggling for a place and refusing to accept their own limits which society does not easily value or tolerate. Since their real gifts and abilities are often ignored by society, the struggle between the search for pleasure in a closed world and the desire to grow in love and service of others is all the more difficult.

In each human being there is an attempt to fill up one's inner void, with things and with power. This is the struggle between egotistical tendencies, 'everything for self', and the opening up of oneself to others. This same struggle goes on in the hearts of those who have learning disabilities.

I believe that the best way for those with learning disabilities to grow in their capacities for work and autonomy is precisely in the acceptance of themselves, with their limits and capacities for growth, through the discovery of their capacities to love and live a real relationship, and communion with others. It is sad when they refuse to face the reality of their disability and withdraw in isolation – for example, by living alone – in order to prove that they are 'like everyone else'.

In l'Arche – and at other centres too – a certain failure with this sort of autonomy has at times been experienced. John, for example, lacking other models, was just looking for a well-paid job and a life where he could do what he wanted. Perhaps he had to acquire this kind of autonomy and the feeling of being 'like everyone else', but the lack of authentic relationships and faithful friends soon reduced his world to work, beer and television. The isolation was perhaps a necessary stage in the discovery of a desire for communion and relationships, with all that implies. I am afraid that many who have milder disabilities tend to close themselves in an autonomy which ends only in such isolation. On the other hand, we have also had some excellent experiences where some of our people have found true autonomy and succeeded in competitive work, but also found peace of heart because they were in a network of good friends.

Developing Confidence

Education consists, therefore, in helping people to discover their capacities and all that is positive and beautiful within them, and to realise that they can establish relationships with others, that they are lovable and able to love. They will discover then the joys of true friendship. They will also discover their human dignity, their capacity to work and to make and do beautiful things. However some of those we have welcomed have such a broken image of themselves that they have no more desire to live. They can fall into self-destructive attitudes. We must offer them a milieu which will call forth what is best in them. Just as some environments call forth darkness and death, so others call forth life and the will to live.

One can deny something to a person only if, at the same time, one conveys an appreciation of and deep confidence in him or her. As discussed earlier, it is the difference between a good shepherd and a hired worker.[1] Then, prohibition can be a sign of hope: 'I know that you can do better.' This presupposes dialogue in which the reason for the prohibition is understood by the one on whom it is imposed. Above all, it is of value when a person has a positive goal in life and can realise that this prohibition will help him or her to become more free and able to choose and find direction in life.

Education consists in giving support to people as they begin to discover the purpose of their lives. There will be times of progress as well as times of failure and discouragement. But, in falling or failing, the person will get up again and there will be the discovery of forgiveness.

I remember a reflection by Dr Franko from whom I asked advice concerning Anthony, a very disturbed man who had committed a serious act with a child: 'You must go to see him and confront him. He may be violent, for it is difficult to accept the darkness which he feels inside. But stay until you have both met and are reconciled. In the past, whenever Anthony did something bad, he was rejected and put in the hospital. It is crucial that he now has an experience of forgiveness.'

It is not easy to educate even a normal child, especially in a society where the values are so often seductive, materialistic and pleasure loving. Parents rarely have the time or the quality of listening necessary to understand their children fully. It is so much easier to put them in front of the television and give them playthings rather than to *play with* them and do things together in joy and celebration. It is difficult for parents not to be possessive with their children or else to use them to satisfy their own emotional needs. It is even more difficult to be a good teacher and to heal the wounded heart of a child with learning disabilities, and to reawaken in him the desire for life.

True Authority

It is not easy to be a good shepherd. I know the theory well and can talk about it. But I realise that often I am more like the 'hired worker' who needs to prove and protect his authority. So often I make quick judgements, forbidding or correcting without taking the time to understand what has really happened. When I correct at an inopportune moment and the correction rebukes rather than helps the other person, my action springs more from my own anguish than from a desire to help the person to grow. This happens most often when I have become overactive, when I have lost the source of light within me, when I am tired, or when I am far removed from the spirit of prayer, being too immersed in the daily concerns without sufficient recollection or inner resources. I know for my part that when it comes to questions of giving or nurturing life in others, it is essential for me to remain close to God through daily prayer.

It is not easy to exercise authority with love and in truth. One has to be firm and clear, and to respect the positive values of the person if one is to find the exact words and gestures which are going to help that person grow. I know my own weaknesses and fears in this respect. But, at the same time, I know the need of those suffering from a disability to have someone who is deeply committed to them in love and respect, yet knowing how to be firm enough to ensure their development and the liberation of their gifts. The one who acts as a shepherd must be a rock of tenderness and truth upon which the other can rely.

I am especially concerned for those who, in their early childhood, had a bad experience with authority. When they have known only prohibitions without kindness or forgiveness, when they have had a rigid education without the stimulation or recognition of their gifts and capacity for growth, they have been deprived of life and development. Sometimes these serious blockages are apparent in their relations with authority, which they regard as a threat to their being. To regain their confidence requires much patience and goodness on the part of the one in authority. The role of the educator, and especially an educator of children and adolescents who have suffered traumas during childhood, requires team work; each one is part of a team and each member is helped to be truthful, and to be true shepherds in their concern for the growth of each person. Each is accountable to the others and so all work closely together. It is very difficult to exercise authority alone; one so quickly becomes defensive or unconsciously oppressive. One tends to protect one's authority and the established order without permitting others to question it.

In order to be objective, a team needs an 'exterior eye', especially when dealing with someone who seems too difficult, disturbed or violent. It is hard to see one's own errors, especially when lack of attention and truthfulness are perhaps at the origins of violence or disruption. In our l'Arche communities it might be the community leader, as distinct from the house leader, who plays this role. On the whole, we prefer it to be someone who has integrated the values of l'Arche within themselves rather than a priest or psychiatrist – someone with experience of the pain and needs of people, someone who has real human wisdom and a knowledge of the Gospels. Priests or ministers and psychiatrists have a major role in the growth and the liberation of the individual and the community; but they must not try to fulfil other roles.

In l'Arche, there is a danger that leaders do not have enough confidence in their own intuition, wisdom and educational abilities; they can submit too passively to 'experts' and professionals. Of course they need to seek advice from others who have greater knowledge and experience, but first of all they must assume their own role in truth and in trust.

Education for Adults

The education of a child is different from that of an adult, even if the latter has a severe intellectual deficiency. An adult, no matter what their abilities or disabilities may be is first of all, an adult, not a child. The body and spirit of a child are still developing, and so the child is naturally accepting and open. The adult already has a story, and the adult with disabilities often has a story of pain and rejection. With a wounded self-image, there is too great a readiness to take the blame. Such a person must be reassured, confirmed and supported. Perhaps there has already been some kind of training in the family or an institution in which different experiences, prohibitions or permissions have left their mark. Pain needs to be healed and bad habits overcome. At the same time, there must be dialogue, the acceptance of failure, and the experience of fragilities, mistakes and limits, in order to go beyond them.

Regarding the emotional and sexual life, the difference between the child and the adult is enormous. The sexuality of the adult is formed, sometimes badly formed, perhaps even perverted, by unhappy experiences in hospital, institution or in a disturbed family situation.

It is not easy to help an adult who has been wounded at the affective level to establish the right distance in a relationship with someone of the other sex. A man who has not been touched with love by his mother, or who has lived a long time in an institutional environment, is scarred in his affectivity. This makes him awkward in being close to or touching a woman, and this awkwardness leads to further rejection.

It is difficult to be close to and touch delicately, with respect and tenderness, men and women who are disturbed. It is important to find ways of touching them in an acceptable manner, for example, when they are sick or complain of a particular pain. Or, it could be through friendly fights or in games and folk dances where there are precise rules about touch that must be respected.

When the values of l'Arche are opposed to the behaviour of the family of the adult with a disability, the situation presents real difficulties. Paul's father, for example, spends much time in bars. Paul loves his father and wants to imitate him. But there is real danger for him. He cannot hold alcohol; his work suffers when he drinks. He senses the conflict between what happens and is accepted at home and what is accepted in l'Arche. Similarly, some men and women go to their families and find their brothers and sisters, and sometimes their parents, having sexual relationships with different partners. It is difficult to let them follow the behaviour of the family with all the likely consequences. How to help them to grow humanly?

We have had successes as well as failures in this domain. Robert, for example, comes from a family where there is much violence and alcoholism. He followed the same route even after he was placed with us. But after several years, he experienced a real healing. With the help of a group similar to Alcoholics Anonymous, he stopped drinking and now actively participates in the group. At some meetings, he testifies: 'I didn't know how I was going to get out of the hell I was in ...' He is proud of his work and lives in a flat with three other men where he has found peace.

Alfred is a man who has certain capacities, but is emotionally disturbed. Refusing all help, he left l'Arche 'to live his own life' and ended up in prison. What will he do when he comes out? Hopefully having hit the bottom, he will be able to accept someone who will help him rise up and give him confidence.

Education for Emotional and Sexual Life

Education for emotional and sexual life means helping someone to have a sense of others, to be able to listen, to love and to have compassion and tenderness and, not least, to become responsible. True sexual education awakens the heart and helps someone move toward a mature affectivity.

This experience of awakening the heart needs a degree of identification with a person of the same sex.

The little boy often imitates his father's relationship with his mother. The way the father acts towards women, especially his wife, will educate most powerfully the sexuality of his son. To some extent the same thing happens in a home for those with disabilities. They will act like the assistants or staff whom they love and admire.

It is through these relationships and the identification with adults that, little by little, people find their own identity. True sexual education takes place in an environment, a home, a network of relationships between men and women, where gestures and touch express joy and tenderness. Sexual education does not occur through anonymous pictures giving depersonalised information. Certainly, it is important to know the anatomy of the body, the times of fertility, the connection between the sexual act and procreation. But it is not always helpful to show the sexual act through pictures or slides because these images risk awakening a sexuality cut off from the life of relationship.

In reality, the role of an educator is to help adolescents understand and appreciate the functions of the body, and to answer their questions. It is serious when a person thinks his or her own body is bad. Counselling engaged couples will, of course, require more precise information as to how a man and woman live their sexuality together. But the emphasis should be on the importance of listening and respecting the differences of the other. Sexual education is not so much a practical manual of what one must do and how, as a basis for harmonious sexual relationship, but rather a matter of helping people to be at ease with their own sexuality. It implies a growth in the capacity to see the other as someone with needs. It also includes helping people to face the challenges and difficulties involved in relationships. This is, in fact, apprenticeship for true love. In most couples it takes a long, long time for one, or both, of the persons to have fulfilling and joyful sexual relationships. Often it is the woman who has the longest period of adjustment. There can be pain involved, or failure to have an orgasm. This can last for years. This is a real learning process that requires much sensitivity towards the other (and most often it is the man who has to learn to be sensitive to the woman's body). It is important for young people to know that sexual relationships don't 'work', are not completely fulfilling, right from the start.

At l'Arche sometimes it is the young assistants who have the most need for sexual education. They have often been so influenced by the mass media which trivialises sexuality and are unable to understand its true significance. They can be afraid of the cry for affection from those with disabilities; they don't know how to respond to manifestations of tenderness or, still less, to manifestations of genital sexuality. Since they themselves are unclear, they are unsure whether to condemn or to ignore what they see.

In our times, we need more than healthy morals in this area of sexual relations. We need a deep understanding of anthropology, which is the foundation of human and Christian ethics. It is necessary to help others to understand how sexual relations without true commitment can quickly become destructive for the human heart and that sexuality must be oriented, elevated and integrated by love, which alone makes it truly human. It is important to learn that this sexuality, prepared by biological and psychic growth, develops harmoniously and is realised in its fullness only by the attainment of emotional maturity, manifested in a selfless love and in the gift of self.

This form of sexual education is equally necessary for men and women with learning disabilities. For them, the influence of films and magazines can sometimes be shattering. The mass media stimulate their sexual instincts, arousing false dreams of 'love'. It is more difficult for them, because their hearts are more fragile than others and they are close to anguish and so easily influenced. They must be able to speak with someone about these questions and come to understand what is at stake in true love. Only then will they be able to make a real choice.

In this area of counselling and education it is imperative that those who accompany people with disabilities are people with the sensitivity and goodness needed to face so much pain, confusion and hurt. Too rigid prohibitions, combined with punishment, can lead to greater guilt and fear. It may aggravate blockages or the search for sex in secret and escape into erotic fantasies, just as total freedom in sexual activity can lead to confusion. Those who accompany others also need to recognise the boundaries of their role. It is not necessary to know everything. There must be respect for the private space and the inner secret of each person's being. It is right to interfere when it is certain that the other is in real difficulty and confusion. The rule is always the same: create a trusting relationship where dialogue is possible and where, little by little, fear disappears. Sometimes it will be a long time before such a relationship is achieved. People need to commit themselves over a period of time and be willing to accept the demands implied in such a commitment.

The exercise of authority and the use of prohibition, or on the contrary, encouragement to 'do what you like', is difficult in the sexual sphere. In fact, each educator has his or her own wounds, difficulties, anguish and struggles. An educator, for example, who is struggling with his own sexual compulsions will probably be more rigid and less sympathetic and understanding of the sexual compulsions of others. It is so difficult to be objective in the area of sexuality where all one's own needs and anguish can be quickly projected. Those who desire 'free' sexuality for themselves may encourage others to the same 'freedom', not because it will help them to grow, but in order to justify and prove that their own attitude is right. Without clarity about one's own sexuality, it is impossible to be clear and true about the sexuality of someone else. Fear of one's own sexuality leads to fear of the sexuality of others and consequently to rigidity. Without the freedom to relate to one's own sexuality, there will almost certainly be misunderstanding of the sexuality of another. Those who do not believe in the possibility of their own growth in this area will never have confidence in the growth of others but will fall into a legal and static vision. Those who do not acknowledge their own weakness will not develop the patience needed to help others to progress and integrate their sexuality into their life of relationships.

Making the Necessary Transition to Growth

As we have seen, children sensing that they are not loved experience emptiness and anguish. Barriers are built around their hearts to repress the pain. To cut oneself off from one's own heart is to cut oneself off also from all that is most profound and intimate within, from the very source of life and love.

Unable to live with others, they seek to escape into cerebral activities, aesthetics, work, immediate pleasure and aggression, or into a world of fantasy, anguish and instability. Love is impossible. The intuition of the heart, which makes us sensitive to others and their needs, and which is the foundation of communion and mutual confidence, is lost.

How can we help people rediscover their source of life and love, their wholeness and centre of unity? They must be helped to descend through all the barriers to the most vulnerable region of the heart. In so doing, they will relive certain anguishes of the past, and certain experiences of hate and revolt born of all their inner suffering.

Contact with the deepest feelings of the heart is often an almost unbearable experience, unless there is a good and competent person who will listen to the cry and carry the suffering with compassion. This person needs to know how to accept the aggression which may erupt and is a necessary passage to a true relationship.

I am more and more convinced that each human being needs to be supported and accompanied in such a way, so as to grow and become more loving, transparent and responsible, and to break out of the prison of fear and anguish. It is not only the person with a disability who needs to be accompanied through these interior transitions, but also the assistants. They, too, have their blockages and barriers and must learn to grow towards an ever more responsible love.

At certain times, someone who can no longer find a way to escape inner conflicts will enter into crisis. A crisis is the revelation of an interior void. This emptiness can be filled ultimately only by an authentic love, a love which comes from God, though it often passes through people. This true love reveals to the person that he or she is not alone but is precious, of value and capable of giving life and of loving. When the sources of life are awakened, there is an experience of wholeness which fills the void which the crisis uncovered.

In demolishing the barriers and rediscovering the sources of life, a measure of inner unity, of integration, is attained. Such transitions imply suffering. But often this suffering is accompanied by a new experience of God in the depths and vulnerability of the heart of the person.

Chapter Three

THE RELATIONSHIP BETWEEN MAN AND WOMAN

Man and Woman in the Vision of God

The difference between man and woman is a radical and fundamental one which permeates the depths of their consciousness and affects all human behaviour. It is at the beginnings of life itself. In Genesis 1:27, it is said that God created human beings in the image of God. God created them male and female, wanting them to be one, to be 'one body' (cf. Genesis 2:24). Man and woman were created to be a gift for each other. They each discover their being in relation to God who created them; each in the image of God, they are called to become like God. Such is their fundamental, ultimate goal in the universe. However, they are also a reflection of the image of God in their union and their unity of love. Each one is with and for the other. Each one discovers his or her self in relationship to the other. Relationship then is at the origin of our being and it is the goal of our unique createdness as we put our gifts and capacities at the service of others.

John Paul II speaks often of the 'sponsal'[1] or 'nuptial' body of man and woman, in order to emphasise that the body of one is made to be united to the other.

> Man and woman, in the mystery of creation, are a mutual gift ... they are united by awareness of the gift; they were mutually conscious of the nuptial meaning of their bodies, in which the freedom of the gift is expressed and all the interior riches of the person as subject are manifested.[2]

[49]

Genesis also shows that when man and woman turned away from God, when God was no longer present in their union, they lost their primal innocence. They then experienced a terrible emptiness within themselves; they knew anguish; they became aware of their nakedness and their inner poverty and brokenness. It was then that the man blamed the woman and sought to dominate her. Their union was broken; they became rivals. They were no longer one body.

Thereafter, men and women turned in on themselves, locking themselves up in a closed world to protect themselves. Then they sought power and possessions to fill their inner emptiness and to turn away from their need for intimacy. It is possible to open ourselves again to one another, to create bonds with one another, to enter the world of love, communion, and gift, of sharing and welcome, only as we are gradually liberated from the powers of egoism that keep us closed up in ourselves.

The attraction that man and woman have for each other calls them to go beyond their isolation that would eventually lead to death. Above and beyond the attraction and the individual choice of one another, there is in the depths of man and woman a desire to give life to a new human being.

If human sexuality is oriented towards intimacy and love, biologically it is orientated to fecundity. Woman's body is made to be the first home for a child. Man's body is made to bring fecundity to the woman.

In women there is the rhythm of fecundity each month, the rhythm of the ripening of the egg which has an impact on her physically and emotionally. Many women live this in an extreme way, with heavy days of menstrual tensions and/or heavy, long bleeding, cramps and nausea. Pregnancy and the care of children demand the greater part of woman's strength and energy on so many levels. Woman is also different from man because she carries in her body a kind of bond with death: her ovaries, given to her since her beginnings, age with her. Her fecundity dies when she reaches her late forties or early fifties. Man, however, always produces new sperm but he does not experience this death of biological fecundity.

What exactly are the consequences of these biological differences in the cultural roles of man and woman? It is not easy to differentiate that which originates in the culture and that which originates biologically, and the link between the two. At the beginning, taking into account the different functions of fecundity and material needs, it was obvious that man should give physical protection, going out to hunt and to fight when necessary, while woman was occupied with the home and the care of the children. This clear division of the roles carried a certain responsibility, peace and harmony. Each one knew what he or she must do; that facilitates unity!

However, as we all know, this role division could also lead to the oppression of women and to domestic violence if the sense of mutual respect and devotion to God as the source of their lives and love are lost. This is what happened and what still happens in certain cultures, where men run the risk of being 'macho'. They have an image of themselves as the 'strong man', no longer devoted to care and concern for the wife, unable to listen to her and her questions but expecting her to be completely at his service, and under his control. Such husbands, having lost touch with their inner source, are wounded and devalued in their own eyes and, filled with anguish, may take to drink, squander the family's money and become violent in their anguish.

One of the big changes in Western industrial and technological society is that the physical strength of men is no longer necessary in order to protect women and children, nor to hunt in order for the family to eat. Women in today's society are perfectly capable of caring for their children and earning a living without any help from men. This complicates unity – the roles are not as clear cut. To remain faithful to one another, or to the family unit, is a choice today, not a necessity. If men and women are to continue living as a couple, it will be because they *want* to and not because they *have* to. That means that each one is called to grow to greater maturity and to accept the transformation that marriage implies.

Difficulties in family life also come from a certain ideal of social success to which the man often feels obliged to conform. All familial and scholastic education is geared toward this professional success, seen as a greater priority even than family life. In these societies a doubt can hang over the value of marriage as a permanent bond. This vision can make both partners feel insecure. The 'working couple' has become a social standard. In Western society today, a woman who stays at home with her children and never works has become a luxury, almost an oddity.

These attitudes may sow seeds of division and mistrust between men and women. One can easily understand that the woman cannot bear oppression and so takes any means to liberate herself from it. She rebels at the idea of being man's plaything or possession, and so refuses all dependence on him. It is understandable that some women go so far as to cut all men out of their lives, striving to be appreciated not for their femininity, but for their intelligence, their professionalism or their artistic abilities. They are obliged to accentuate their aggressiveness and their desire for success, and they tend to deny the sensitivity of their hearts which, like man's, are made for communion and mutual dependence. They seem to be driven, in an attempt to defend themselves, to adopt the same false model of masculinity, which is oriented towards individual success. It is important however to affirm that women are as equally competent as men, and in many instances, more so. Their intellectual capacities, linked to a deep, inner wholeness, can make them highly qualified.

Couples' preoccupation with financial gain and professional success, together with other factors such as the role of the mass media, have considerably weakened the family. The idea of service has been partially destroyed. We have over-developed individualism as a necessity for life and success. The bonds which unite people in the family, the community, the parish and the village tend to disintegrate. People are more and more isolated from each other. A vicious circle is created and one must harden oneself in order to survive. As 'the body' which is the family, the village, the community has been weakened, people who are non-productive and fragile (whether due to a disability, age or ill-health) have difficulty in finding their place in such a society. They are quickly rejected or simply left by the wayside. In a society where individualism is so highly valued, life becomes a battle. It is necessary to be the best at something in order to achieve meaning: if one is not the best, then one is good for nothing. This leads people to look down on others, scorning those who are not successful.

The Christian vision of the human being is very different from that of our industrial societies. The Word, becoming flesh, came to reveal the great dignity of *each person*, above all the poorest and the weakest, and to call them to live in a community which is united like a body. The last are first. The values of the Christian vision are neither power, nor social influence, nor riches, nor human glory, nor even individual liberty as an end in itself. Its values are those of love exercised in the 'body' of community, which is the Church.

In the perspective of Jesus, the weakest ones are the most important because they have the greatest need to be loved, protected and served; their cry is for relationship. 'Blessed are the poor, for the kingdom of heaven is theirs.' The leaders, those responsible in the Church, are there to serve them, to wash their feet. God chose the weak to confound the strong, the foolish to confound the wise, the scorned to confound the proud. Jesus blessed his Father for having hidden these things from the wise and the prudent, from the intellectuals and the rich, and for having revealed them to the poor. So it is that the Church is called to be evangelised by the weak. The Church needs their gifts of love. It is the weak who lead the strong and the so called wise to compassion and to service and to Jesus. Isn't that why Paul says that those who are weak are 'necessary' to the Body, which is the Church (cf. 1 Corinthians 12).

Whenever there is a perversion, whenever the body is broken, when man does not give woman her due, when the poor are not respected, it is difficult to retrieve the situation. I can understand the anger and suffering of so many women. What is to be done now? Is it really possible to continue living, as many do today, in this dynamic based on aggression and individualism? Or is it possible, through recognition of and respect for differences, to rediscover the deepest community values of trust and mutual support?

In the following chapter, I speak of the home. Today, when one speaks of the values of the home, men are bored and women get angry as if one wished to send them back to the kitchen and housework without any contact with the world outside. However, it is important to speak of the home, because in our times many families are broken, and so many children live with a sense of being abandoned and isolated and are in anguish. They have to harden themselves in order to survive, and their hearts, the most sensitive part of their being, can be smothered, if not crushed. It seems to me that the most fundamental need of our society is not to have more teachers in universities, but to have men and women who together create communities of welcome for those who are rejected, alone and lost – and their number is legion. It is more than ever essential to rediscover the sense of home as a place of tenderness and welcome, where each one can find the deepest value of his or her being – the heart with its capacity to receive and to give. Today many people wish to become involved in society, but they live all alone and sometimes in conflict with others. They have neither community nor family as a source of personal nourishment, tenderness and peace.

I am convinced that our society desperately needs the reconciliation between men and women in order to build community together. They have such need of each other, and it is painful and even dangerous when they lose mutual respect and appreciation of one another.

It is obvious that women and men are equally competent. Within l'Arche, women are responsible for some of our communities, men for others. Women, for the most part, exercise authority differently from men, neither better nor worse. At certain times in the history of a community, it might be better to have a man carrying the responsibility; at other times a woman. The essential is that neither exercises authority alone. Woman need to remain partners with man, and man with woman. This complementarity is healthy and valuable.

In my experience, I have found that usually the man has a better sense of means, of organisation, of structure. The woman is often more intuitive and her heart is frequently more sensitive; she has a better sense of ultimate objectives and of people. This is not to say that every community must comprise both men and women, or that a community of only men or only women will never be successful. If all the members of a community are of the same sex, then it is important that the leader of the community shares responsibility with others who in some way bring in this complementarity. There are of course some men who are more intuitive and some women who have an excellent sense of organisation.

Each of us, according to life, circumstances and inner disposition, may develop more of our 'feminine' qualities (those which touch intuition, welcome, tenderness, caring) or more of our 'masculine' qualities (those related to reason and organisation). When necessary, men can be sensitive to the body and express great tenderness, just as women can be hard and aggressive. The important thing, in a family as in a larger community, is that each one is able to use his or her own gifts, knowing that the gifts of one are not better than the gifts of another, that each one at his own level participates in decisions, that each one listens to the others and cares for their well-being. That is the joy of community. In general, male energy is a creative force that is directed, goal-oriented, focused, productive and stands alone from the whole. Female energy is an inward-drawing energy that is unstructured, all-encompassing, oceanic, and does not differentiate or individualise. Female energy conditions the environment, while male energy structures it. Men and woman contain both of these energies. One is more dominant but both are available to every person.

Given the specific purpose of l'Arche, namely the welcome of people who have been wounded in their minds and in their hearts, we need both men and women assistants. They play complementary roles in the healing and growth of people with disabilities, provided that they love one another and cooperate together.

Accepting Differences

The family is the primal community. It is founded on difference between men and women and on the recognition of each by the other. Both are with and for their children. Children are also different but not inferior. They do not have the power of adults, and bring their unique gifts to the family and to the community. They are more than just potential adults. They are people in their own right.

There is a tendency today to deny differences. This tendency is the basis of most sects, in contrast to the basis of community. A sect always wants uniformity, even a form of fusion, because this gives greater security. The leader has absolute power and is regarded as a unique and inspired prophet, even like a god. He or she is the sole reference, demanding unquestioning obedience. The goal of community, on the other hand, is the freedom and growth of each person. It implies the recognition of committed relationships but in diversity. In community there is a mutual bond which still leaves each member free to grow in his or her differences.

To feel lonely and isolated because of being different is a terrible human suffering. Peace lies in the recognition of the value of differences. When someone feels alone, they barricade themselves behind walls to suppress the pain. However when a person feels accepted by others it is possible to drop defences and enter confidently into relationships with others. When bonds become firmly established community is born.

The Scandinavian countries introduced the notion of 'normalisation' for people who have a disability. This concept has value, if we understand it to mean that each person has rights and that no one must be excluded from the human community because of a disability. But, if by 'normalisation' we mean that everyone is 'normal', that everyone must be the same, then we tend to deny differences, and this is wrong. The 'Normalisation Principal' of Wolf Wolfensburger states that people should have the right to live in society in 'normal' circumstances, but with the necessary accompaniment – and not be forced to live in abnormal circumstances, such as institutions, or in homes of 30 or 40 people, simply because they are disabled. While we would not want to generalise, it is true that people with learning disabilities are different from others; they need help in certain areas. It is also true that each one has needs and gifts which are their own. What is important is that these gifts and these needs be acknowledged and that each person is able to find their place in the human community.

My forty-two years of living together in l'Arche, with men and women who have disabilities, has taught me that the deepest longing of each one is to create bonds and to live with others in the spirit of a family. They do not want to live simply with professionals who, notwithstanding their goodness and competence, get paid for putting in their hours of work and then leave. They wish to live in true bonds of friendship with others.

When for ideological reasons we cannot accept people who are different, but reject them or wish they were not present, we are forcing them to be other than they are. Only when differences are accepted, as a treasure and not as a threat, are people enabled to be more freely and fully themselves.

Acceptance of difference, however, requires a maturity of heart and spirit that human beings do not possess straight away. Instead of an authentic acceptance of the other, there is often the search for a symbiotic unity: 'We love each other', 'We are one'; but without truly respecting the other in his or her differences and need to grow. Respect implies dialogue. It implies that we give others the space they need to live and grow freely, that we do not invade their frontiers. The demands of recognising another person in this way are onerous and can be a terrible challenge, bringing suffering with growth.

In order to find one's space one often has to cry out or even fight for recognition. That can hurt those close by and arouse their anger. The search for symbiotic unity often comes from a fear of this anger. On the other hand, when differences are respected then the potential for aggression diminishes. If we want others to live, we must not try to manipulate them or control them. We need to give them more space; and that can involve loss and pain for ourselves.

In order to accept this loss and all that resembles death, there must be, as I said in the first chapter, a new inner strength, a transformation, which often comes from the experience of God's love. With faith in a transcendent being, it is perhaps easier to welcome differences, and beyond that, to create real community, a 'body', where each person accepts the other and recognises their need for the special gifts the others have to bring to the body as a whole.

The community needs those special gifts which are especially man's and those which are especially woman's; it needs the gifts of the child and those of the elderly; it also needs the gifts of those with disabilities. In the same way, the world community needs all men and all women, all races and all nations.

Mixed Homes

A milieu with both men and women is the best and truest one for someone with a disability – and maybe this is true for all of us. Quite often, it is the woman who calls forth in a man that which is most profound: the heart, tenderness and sensitivity. The man thus becomes more gentle, more attentive, more discerning. He opens himself more to others. The woman awakens his goodness, just as the man awakens all that is most beautiful and feminine in the woman. Man and woman are as mirrors to each other; their differences reveal to each other who he or she is. This permits each one to be himself or herself in his masculinity or her femininity. In a mixed milieu, work must be shared according to tastes and aptitudes; men and women more naturally find their own place, but not determined entirely by their gender, and through that, assume a clearer responsibility.

A man does not always call forth the best in a woman, nor a woman that which is best in a man. The male presence may awaken in a woman the desire to seduce, to play one man against another and so to create discord. She may awaken in a man real sexual obsessions. In one of our communities, a man who was actually quite mentally ill was so disturbed by the presence of women that he became quite violent. He found peace in an institution where there were only men.

For some men and women, because of their early childhood, mixed homes can be unhealthy. They can reawaken such instincts of fear and dependence and destruction that it becomes impossible for them to live close to the opposite sex. As we have said, there is in some people such a fear of love! I remember a prisoner saying to me, 'When someone is brutal with me, I know how to react; but, when someone is kind or tender toward me, I am lost.'

Some men and women have erected such enormous barriers around their vulnerable hearts, and have so learned to live with them, that attempts to remove these barriers can be dangerous if one is not an experienced, professional therapist. At l'Arche, we have met men and women suffering from 'hospitalisation', having lived for many years in institutions in a kind of anonymity with strict discipline. They are not able to live in a family setting where they are given freedom and are constantly faced with choices. They prefer a more structured life, less threatening to them. But, perhaps, more deeply they are afraid of the pain hidden behind the fortifications of their heart. They are afraid of awakening sexual compulsions which might be accompanied by obsessions and jealousies, or by a desire to hurt and wound because the one whom they love is not exclusively theirs and theirs alone. If, in childhood, they have not had a special relationship with their parents, anything which awakens the desire to be unique could become a dangerous mixture of trust and fear, love and hate.

In most of the l'Arche communities throughout the world, men and women live together. I can say that on the whole, this seems to be very positive, bringing peace and harmony and helping most residents to integrate their sexual urges. In those homes where there are only men or only women, there appears to be more aggression. Mixed homes are more human, because people

in them seem to be kinder and more sensitive towards one another. Nevertheless, it is still true that for some it is better to live
in separate homes for men or for women alone.

Sources of Relationship

If, out of fear, someone is not able to live a personal relationship
of communion and gift, a friendship, with someone of the other
sex, he or she will inevitably be disturbed at the level of genital
sexuality. This is why, if we wish to understand the emotional and
sexual life of someone, we have to go back to the origins of his or
her relationship with the father and mother.

I was surprised one day when speaking with Pierrette, a young
Canadian delinquent. She appeared to be very tough. She loved to
wear leather belts and ride powerful motorcycles. But, behind this
façade of toughness was a sensitive heart capable of true love. She
confided to me, however, that when she hated a man she went to
bed with him. She delighted in having him at her mercy, weak,
begging for her body. It was evident that unconsciously she was
taking revenge on her father who was very weak, an alcoholic who
never gave her the love and tenderness she needed when she was
a child.

The relationship of the little boy with his mother, like that of
the little girl with her father, conditions the relationships which,
when the child becomes an adult, he or she will have with those
of the other sex. Certainly, as we have said earlier, it is not a question of separating the relationship of the child with one parent
from the relationship with both parents. He or she needs both. If
these relationships have been positive, the adolescent will have
fewer difficulties with whoever will be his or her spouse. A child
who has lived with many foster or stepmothers is likely to have
difficulties later on in living in a permanent relationship.
Sometimes, adults have a tendency to unconsciously re-enact the
conflicts and sufferings they knew as children. In fact, the fears and
traumas of childhood condition future relationships. They often
remain hidden in the unconscious, and certain events tend to

reawaken them.

Karl Stern in his book *Flight from Woman*[3] shows that some disturbed men either put woman on a pedestal – idealising her, seeing her as a model of purity – or they see her as the prostitute, the temptress. They are incapable of a simple relationship, one to one, with her. This inability to see her as a friend is not primarily a rejection of women, but a rejection of their own disturbed genital sexuality.

When a boy, abandoned by his mother, has not experienced the warmth and bodily affection he needs, his body cries out for the touch of a woman-mother. This is the case of George who lives in one of our communities: he had an almost uncontrollable need to touch and caress women, to attract them to him. His need to touch and be touched was not primarily a genital sexual need. It was not in the literal sense a sexual urge; it was a cry of his deprived body longing to be loved and appreciated by a woman-mother. The deprivation of touch has long lasting effects on the body.

George greatly annoyed women, who did not like to be touched in this way, since his attraction towards them could be interpreted as sexual. Some psychologists get people with this kind of difficulty to regress to babyhood in the arms of a substitute mother. But this can be dangerous, for, while it is easy enough to lead some who have lacked love during childhood to this type of regression, it is much more difficult to bring them back from this situation. Such wounded people want to remain at this level, demanding more and more, an unfailing love without limits, and thus an impossible love.

It is important that the team around George should understand that he is seeking a mother and not a wife. It is dangerous when these two aspects become confused. In order for George to grow, he needs to live a harmonious and peaceful relationship with a woman who will not awaken his genital sexuality but who will pacify him and give him security and peace. He needs to find a woman who knows how to make maternal gestures, who knows how to take care of his body without putting him in danger, who knows how to care for him and his clothing, who knows how to spoil him sometimes. However, it is also necessary that this substitute mother is not the only one concerned with George and that she knows when to absent herself in order to avoid awakening in him a too great attachment to her which could be harmful. George also needs to relate to men, who will serve as models in their healthy relationship with women. If George is surrounded by such a team, perhaps his heart will begin to grow towards peace and maturity.

Many seem to ignore the fact that, underlying the sexual drive, there is, in the sexual attraction, the simple cry of a body longing to be loved and touched with tenderness by another. This cry comes from the depths of a human being and most often has its origins in childhood. The links which unite genital sexuality and this call to be loved, held and caressed are so profound that sometimes they lead a person to a state of confusion and fear. The cry for relationship gets mixed up with sexual desire. A person may then be very afraid of relationships, especially if their experiences of sexual urges have been disturbing. Such is the case of a man I know who had been put in a psychiatric hospital for many years because he had molested a girl. Thus can arise a fear of all relationship with the other sex; the person may then escape into other activities to shield the heart. This often creates attitudes of domination or aggression.

This escape can be positive in a way; the person deeply recognises that their call to be loved is so intense as to be too dangerous and too confused. When one is a fully grown adult, one can no longer play at being a little helpless baby. Those who have difficulties in relating must learn to accept them. They must try to distance themselves from their own cry to be loved. A community life where relationships are more structured is more appropriate to their needs. There they will be able to channel their energies into leisure activities, work and service to others.

Today there is a danger of thinking that everyone can become perfectly healed and find perfect unity, in themselves and with others. Personally, I am more and more convinced that there is no perfect healing. Each human being carries his or her own wounds, difficulties of relationship and anguish. It is a question of learning to live day after day with this reality and not in a state of illusion, and to accept the necessary help in order to become more emotionally mature. We must also learn to accept who we are and live with what we have, focusing our strength on those others who are in greater need and sometimes in deep distress.

Emotional Maturity and Immaturity

I often hear people say that someone with an intellectual disability has a normal sexuality. This is true if we look at genital sexuality as no more than a physical and biological reality, separated from the person in his or her totality. But is it possible to separate the genital sexuality of a person from the need for love and the capacity to assume responsibility for another person? For surely it is in the emotional needs and capacities for responsibility that the difference can appear between someone with a learning disability and someone who has a developed intelligence and capacity to reason and who can be responsible for themself and for others.

In order to live a deep relationship, including sexuality in its more physical aspects, it is necessary for each person to have a certain degree of emotional maturity and to be capable of exercising responsibility and fidelity towards another. Young people who enter into sexual relationships without having a certain emotional maturity can do harm to themselves and to their partners. They carry in their bodies and in their psyches realities they are unable to integrate into their affectivity. Precocious sexual experience can often hinder the necessary process of maturation of the personality and later on make fidelity to one person difficult.

People with learning disabilities often have enormous emotional needs. It would be erroneous to believe that gestures of tenderness and affection spring solely from a need for genital sexuality. My forty-two years of experience in l'Arche have shown me the contrary. Some people interpret these gestures as though they are leading to an expression of genital sexuality, which frightens them. In many of these situations, these are natural and spontaneous gestures which simply express: 'I like you. I like being with you.' In some cases, it is true, these gestures may also be an imitation of what has been seen in films.

Of course, there are those people who are more developed and who seek an expression of their genital sexuality. They need to be helped to grow towards a greater emotional maturity which will allow them eventually to form a real relationship of friendship with a view to marriage.

Many people with learning disabilities have undoubtedly a great wealth of the heart. Their love, in its simplicity and tenderness, gives them an extraordinary liberty with regard to established conventions. How many times we have seen someone with disabilities greet visitors to L'Arche by saying: 'What's your name? What do you do? Will you give me your necktie?' A grown-up girl with Down's syndrome can look at a man with great tenderness and take his hand, or throw herself into his arms. If she did not have a disability, such an overture and lack of reserve would probably be interpreted by the man as an invitation to more physical union. But this is not the case. Her tenderness does not necessarily imply a search for a sexual relationship.

Her tenderness and her call for tenderness are terribly disarming; because she has the body and the beauty of a woman, she is able to arouse the sexuality of a man. Alas, it is not surprising that men and women with disabilities are so often abused. In a little pamphlet published in the State of Washington, USA (population about 4,000,000), it is estimated that in this state no less than 30,000 mentally or physically disabled people are sexually abused each year.[4] This is a startling revelation of the suffering, loneliness and anguish of those people who abuse them and of the pain and fragility of those who are abused!

Some people with Down's syndrome express their desire to marry their helper or teacher. We should not be surprised by this; many little boys want to marry their teachers. A four-year-old boy can also want to marry his mother! This reflects a desire for total oneness with her, a fear of being separated from her — a fear of growing up. Such fears are linked to deep anguish. We find similar characteristics in those with a profound disability and with an immaturity comparable to that of a child. It is normal that a young woman with disabilities falls in love with a male assistant or a young man with a female assistant.

A young man and woman with disabilities may be attracted in some way to each other but that does not mean that they should be encouraged to have a sexual relationship or to marry. If there is immaturity such a relationship would lack any sense of the responsibility that such a relationship entails. To encourage a sexual relationship could simply aggravate their immaturity.

Over the years, at l'Arche, we have lived a variety of experiences which reveal the different forms this emotional immaturity may take. Edith, a young woman of 22, is very seductive. She desperately seeks men and loves to see them fight over her. She provokes rivalry and jealousy. It is clear that she needs to grow and find greater maturity. She has not yet attained even the stage of a simple or healthy friendship.

In another l'Arche community, Micheline, a young psychotic woman, has totally captivated Bernard. He follows her around like a puppy. It is evident that the bond which unites them is unhealthy and not at all liberating for either of them. They are closed in on each other.

Francis seeks a liaison with a girl because his mother is convinced he will be healed if he sleeps with a woman. So he is seeking a relationship with a woman, but in response to his parent's desire, not his own. He is still only a child in some ways.

When someone has a broken or negative self-image and does not love their own body, it is impossible to love the body of another in a healthy way. Some women find pleasure and excitement in attracting or seducing men. They are terribly lonely and sad women who crave to be loved, but are afraid of not being truly lovable. Through their bodies they seek to attract men and awaken their sexuality, but they are afraid of real relationship and commitment. It is important to prevent other people who are terribly immature from falling into the snare of seduction and relationships which may hurt and disappoint them.

Emotional immaturity is simply a yearning to be loved, to be touched, to be at the centre, to be seen as unique, but without making the effort to love, without a willingness to assume responsibility for the other. It is a desire for a totally consuming relationship, linked to a fear of separation and growing up.

This immaturity arises most often when there has been no true paternal presence. If the mother's role is to cultivate tenderness and a sense of being wanted and loved, the father's is to call the child to growth, to love and serve others in their turn.[5] This is why a real education implies the presence of both parents. The mother says: 'I love you. Stay with us.' The father says: 'I love you. I am proud of you. You are capable of doing beautiful things, of making others happy, Go …' Of course, we must not be rigid in fixing roles. Each in some way assumes both roles, but generally speaking each accentuates one aspect.

What is important is that we do not confuse the immature call of someone who wants to be loved with the desire for a sexual relationship. We must distinguish between the desire to find a mother who comforts and the desire to have a wife. A marriage in which the man is searching more for a mother than a wife often breaks apart when he discovers his responsibilities as a husband. To enter into sexual relationships when one is at this stage of immaturity can hinder growth to the ultimate stage where one becomes capable of loving, of serving, and of being responsible for the other. This is why it is dangerous to introduce people too early into a world where they experience sexual relations without responsibility.

Sexual Abuse [6]

Sexual abuse is a gruesome reality. Abuse of all kinds is particularly a danger for people with learning disabilities, or any vulnerable person. Sexual predators, wounded themselves, methodically seek out and groom vulnerable victims, first establishing their trust, and then horrendously betraying it. One result of such violation is that individuals who have been rejected or abused as children, emotionally or physically or sexually, often lack appropriate boundaries, for either healthy intimacy or appropriate self-protection. This puts them at higher risk as adults for predators seeking vulnerable adult victims.

At l'Arche as elsewhere, people with learning disabilities have lived stories of abuse and re-abuse in families and institutions, and this profoundly affects their relationships and healing journey in community. The coping skills which helped the victim survive the abuse as a child may interfere with healthy day to day functioning in the here and now. Difficult behaviour may often be best understood in this light.

What is clear, however, is that the sexual impulse that is not infused with an authentic love and a real desire for the other person to be and to grow humanly and spiritually, can be terribly dangerous. Erotic literature, films and publicity seek to excite this sexual impulse which can then 'take over' people and lead them into perverse and dangerous acts, using another person for one's own sexual pleasure. To proclaim that these impulses must be 'liberated' is folly because it can lead to wounding people and particularly children, in a horrendous way. A sexuality that is not educated and orientated to giving life to another and sealed in a covenant relationship, reveals itself as a broken sexuality.

Sexual abuse may be inflicted by a same-sex predator, instilling in the victim anguish and confusion about his or her own orientation. This should be kept in mind when these are manifested within the community setting.

The Implications for l'Arche

Many of the men and women welcomed at l'Arche have lived through painful human situations. They have experienced long periods in psychiatric hospitals or other institutions. Perhaps these times of institutionalisation could not have been avoided. So many families are unable to respond to the needs of their children in times of great difficulty. During these periods these young people perhaps came to know a staff of educators and nurses who really cared for them with great competence and goodness. However core members are often marked also by deep suffering at the level of their emotions and by the painful question as to why they were abandoned and removed from their family. It was during these times at the hospital that some men and women were perhaps sexually abused. Such situations are particularly sad and are the most delicate to deal with. We must help these men and women to find freedom from these tendencies which close them in upon themselves. We must help them to transcend the terrible injustices of the past.

Those who suffer certain inner brokenness and terrible crises of anguish are very fragile. The spirit and mind become confused and all sense of responsibility can be lost. Such people are easily manipulated and are unable to take control of their own lives. They seek desperately to calm their inner agitation by every possible means. One of these means is the exercise of genital sexuality, whether alone or with others of the same sex. If this happens, it is very difficult to free someone from sexual habits once they are established and impressed into the flesh, precisely because they are directly related to the anguish of an unfilled hunger to be loved and touched and have become a form of addiction. These habits give a certain appeasement to that inner agitation for a short time. There is a feeling of calm relaxation and well-being.

This cry of those who have a terrible need to be touched, to be loved and to experience intimacy with someone can become so intense that they are pulled irresistibly into sexual relations. But it is not so much the sexual relation and the pleasure attached to a sexual act as such which is important to them, but a feeling of togetherness, through the proximity of bodies, which appeases their anguish.

It is evident that liberation from being physically and emotionally enslaved by sexual impulses, like all liberation from the weight of egoism and self-centredness and addictions, can only come after much struggle and effort, undergone with the support of a community life and real friendship, and accompanied with sensitivity and dedication by professionals, priests and ministers. Perhaps liberation will come only after many failures, setbacks and sufferings, and after many reconciliations and rebirths.

Masturbation

The danger of masturbation is that it can become an obsession, taking over from real relationship, encouraging isolation and fantasy. As with other kinds of genital sexuality, the modern tendency is to trivialise it: 'It is not important. It is normal, simply a question of adolescence. It will pass. Do not make a fuss about it.' It is important, however, to try to understand some of the mechanisms behind this need to masturbate.

Adolescence is of crucial importance, because it is the time of growth to sexual maturity. That maturity is shown in a real commitment towards others, a commitment which is not just a running away from one's own suffering into the outside world, but one which springs from inner peace, harmony and the search for unity and truth within. Jesus said: 'Blessed are the pure of heart, they will see God.' That purity is a quality of love in the sense that one speaks of 'pure' gold. It is the fire and intensity of love, of service, of humility, of patience, and of goodness. Thus, to the extent that adolescents struggle for this purity of love, they will progress towards a true maturity and will be able to assume responsibility in the deepest struggles of our world.

The other day, I was told of a thirty-year-old woman who has had great difficulties with masturbation ever since she was seven. She could not overcome these tendencies and lived with feelings of enormous guilt. It is probable that at the age of seven this young woman had lived, through a traumatic experience, now hidden in the unconscious, that caused terrible anguish. It was this which made her take refuge in masturbation; it brought a certain calm to her inner agitation. Now, on the conscious level, there is a habitual link between the experience of anguish and masturbation.

Masturbation can tend to close the person up inside a dream world. The maturity of a person is manifested by a capacity to face reality, to cope with it, and really to love and serve people just as they are and not as we want or imagine them to be. Because of this, masturbation can become a sexual experience that is more satisfying and less complicated than sexual activity with another person. A young, married women told me once about her young husband who would be in the bathroom masturbating with a sex magazine, while she was waiting, frustrated, for him to make love to her in the bedroom. The marriage didn't last long.

When masturbation begins at an early age, there is a danger of the person being trapped in a genital sexuality directed not towards communion with another and the gift of oneself to another, but towards a subjective pleasure for oneself. Furthermore, masturbation being a solitary act, can reinforce fear of relationships with others. It then becomes a vicious circle: masturbation aggravates isolation and increases loneliness and thus brings more anguish, which the person then seeks to alleviate by masturbation. The aim of education is to liberate the person from such an impasse.

I wrote earlier about Gloria. Her parents considered her mad, but men in the area desired her. She left prostitution but there remained within her terrible struggles and compulsions. The assistants in her community have been able to stop her from masturbating in public. But at night, she manipulates her body in masturbation. For the moment, the assistants say nothing about this because she cannot handle too many prohibitions at a time. She is beginning to trust the assistants and to feel at home. This is an enormous step. With time, it is probable that the anguish will diminish. The assistants have also decided to give her something to help her sleep because the anguish at night is sometimes too awful. If she is able to sleep better over a length of time, this will help her to break the habit, because there will be less experience of anguish. What is important is for the assistants to accentuate all that is positive in her, all that gives her life and joy, all that awakens new and constructive energies in her, all that will bring her security and the feeling of being loved.

In our communities, we have also young men with disabilities who were attracted by children, either to touch them sexually or to show them their genital organs. These situations are rare, but they do exist and call for enormous vigilance. We must protect children from such traumatic experiences and we need to help people with disabilities to find healing. We also need to protect the community, for these situations could create a scandal with the neighbours and a court action against the community. When I visited prisons, I met men who had been sentenced for sexual crimes and were often persecuted by other prisoners because of them. I am very moved by the suffering of these young men who are unable to control their sexual impulses and who must spend long years of their lives in prison because of them. At the root of their wounded sexuality there is often a story of rejection and sexual abuse during their childhood, a broken family and a break with the father. Alas, it is always the same story …

Paedophilia, pornography, prostitution and other sexual disorders show how deep the division is in us between the sexual urge and the capacity to live a committed relationship. The sexual urge becomes such an addiction that it cuts people off from reality, and particularly from the reality of the needs of another person. It can lead them to wound other people deeply and to lock themselves up in their own addiction.

Men and Women Caught Up in Prostitution

I had occasion to speak with Father André Marie Talvas, who founded a movement in France for the reintegration of men and women who have been involved in prostitution. His movement, called 'le Nid' (the Nest), began when Father Talvas met a woman in distress in 1937. She lived alone, was sick, an alcoholic and rejected by others. He did not want to leave her in her loneliness. Gradually she found life through him. Now, throughout all the big cities of France, 'le Nid' comes to the aid of those living in prostitution and other marginal people. Father Talvas knows a lot about prostitution and the suffering and needs of these men and women. He confirmed deeply my own understanding of the emotional and the sexual life. 'God's plan for humankind', he told me, 'is to participate in the life of God – Father, Son and Holy Spirit. It is to communicate with another; it is to love. The greatest tragedy for a human being is to be locked up in oneself and unable to communicate. So many of the women I know did not receive their share of love when they were little. A person who has not received her share of love, will never be able to have her share of life.'

This is the suffering of men and women reduced to slavery and considered as objects. Yet there is also the suffering of their clients. 'Most of them', Father Talvas said, 'are searching not so much for sexual pleasure as for tenderness and communication. Often it is the poorly loved who seek for someone who will listen to them and welcome them. We cannot separate genital sexuality from the heart and the emotions. Beneath the search for genital sexuality is a longing to be loved. One seeks it where one can. We must help these clients – as well as the pimps and go-betweens – to find the true life of a couple which is at the heart of the true life of a family.'

In order to be liberated from prostitution a man or woman needs to find someone who will really respect and care for him or her, and will recognise what is truly precious and beautiful in them. Andrée, a victim of prostitution herself, said she was liberated when she experienced for the first time in her life that someone cared for her.[7]

Growth

After all these years in l'Arche, living with men and women who are often quite disturbed, I know how important it is to be aware of all the nuances and complexities in this area of healing and education. We have experienced failures, yet each one has taught us something; the pain, the anguish of each person in distress is so different. It is true that there are basic patterns which are constant, but at the same time we recognise that there are no fixed or precise laws. This is the reality of each human person and of his or her growth.

In order to grow, each person needs to be surrounded by friends and to be regarded as full of potential for growth. Deficiencies of love in early childhood play an enormous role in a social and maladjusted behaviour. But sometimes chemical deficiencies accompany affective deficiencies. It is evident that there is an intimate link between the physical and the psychological.

Inner liberty and the attitude of those around us as well as an individual's psychology and experience of faith, are all interrelated. We cannot say that the disturbance in a person comes solely from a lack of spirituality or fidelity, from a deprivation of love, or a chemical deficiency requiring medication. Anguish is a complex reality that all of us experience from time to time and which has a physical basis as well as psychological and spiritual elements. For the heart and the person to be on the road to healing there must be a gentle and subtle harmonisation of these different aspects.

Chapter Four

A PLACE FOR THE HEART

Activities of the Heart and Activities of Work

A duality exists between man and woman as they are called to form, from their two distinct bodies, one flesh. This is similar, in a way, to a duality which exists in each of us between the activities of the heart and the activities of work, which must be united in one person.

We have seen that passion for work may come from fleeing the insecurity and fear with regards to the demands of the heart or of genital sexuality. Work can be an escape, a compensation for the anguish that arises from not being able to cope with the demands of relationship: trust, openness, reciprocity, belief in oneself and the other. It can spring from isolation and lead to isolation. When individuals have no confidence that they are looked upon and have been chosen as unique in love, they may seek to be unique or admired in power, domination or other domains, or else they may fall into sadness and depression. When the heart is denied or when people think that love involves simply creating a dependency or seeking control over another, there is a risk of giving primacy to struggle or competition in which it is necessary to win at all costs. Sadly, in order to be first, one has to step on and trample over others. It is hard then to be in a relationship of equality; either one has to be superior, or one is automatically inferior.

The role of ethics is to orient human activities to the service and the well-being of others. Activities would otherwise be inspired by egoism and a growing preoccupation with oneself, one's own power and pleasure.

There is certainly a danger at the present time, and perhaps at all times, of separating the sphere of the heart and the sphere of work. In the family we live relationships of love and we even accept that morality and religion have a place there. However, we do not easily accept the intervention of religion and morality in the areas of work and of the sciences. In these domains, the brutal logic of facts reigns supreme, without regard to whether they crush or oppress. This alienation of intellect from soul reinforces a breakdown in the human being, and fails to move humanity towards the restoration of unity.

In l'Arche, some men and women with disabilities grow towards a human equilibrium through work and professional activity, which give them a sense of their responsibility and dignity as workers. It is only in discovering this dignity of their being that they are able to advance towards a healing of their hearts. There are others, however, who must move to a healing of their hearts before being able to discover their ability to assume responsibility at work.

At Home

In order to attain a certain fullness and maturity, the human person has need of both work and a family. Work is the place where one's intellectual and manual abilities are exercised for some useful and, hopefully, beautiful purpose. The family, or community, is the place where the heart can flourish. It is home, with all the nuances which that word carries, that is so much more than walls of a house. It is 'my place', which implies security, privacy and, above all, relaxation and friendship. In work, there are inevitably tensions, for there is a finished product to be made, and perhaps an agenda or discipline to be respected. At home, one can relax, rest and find nourishment. One can be at ease with others, who do not judge or demand too much. They can communicate tenderness and friendship and allow one to be oneself. Home is the place of the family, where people love each other, pray and celebrate together. It is a place to welcome friends.

Human beings come from the earth and return to the earth. They follow the rhythm of nature, in which there is day and night, work and rest, a time to be nourished and a time to exert energy. There is the daily routine of work and times of celebration. There is winter, spring, summer and autumn. Each time, like each season, is important. Human beings are not disembodied spirits, but have bodies subject to the laws of nature.

I must admit that as I share my life with people who have a learning disability, they are leading me into the discovery of my own humanity. As a naval officer, I had to be quick and efficient. In war you have only seconds to sink the enemy ship before being sunk yourself. Later I obtained a doctorate in philosophy which formed my intellect. However, it was only through living in a community and deepening my Christian faith that I began to discover all the dimensions of my heart. In this area, those with a disability were truly my masters, my teachers. They led me to discover the beauty, joys and pain of community life, with the daily routine of work and of celebrations. They helped me to discover the value of 'home'.

The home is an extension of the body, a place where one is revitalised and where one communicates with others. If home is a place of conflict, where no one shares or communicates with others, it is intolerable. One has to run away somewhere: perhaps to a bar, to other places of leisure, to another's home, or into conjugal infidelity.

My experience has shown me how important the woman is in the creation of home. Woman has a profound sense of the nest – she carries her child within her for nine months. For example, she may have an intuitive sense of the right décor and furniture for the house that a man does not always have. Often she has the special gift of giving the house a soul.

Unfortunately, in our era and in Western civilisation, we attach great importance to having a beautiful house – beautiful at least to the outward eye – a house where one's possessions are safe, but which often lacks a certain quality of family life. Then the house is no longer a place of celebration and tenderness, where one loves to welcome others and make them feel at home. The house is then like a boarding house or showcase, without soul, without heart. We long to leave to go on holidays or to outside entertainment. Often, when we are too tired to share with each other and have lost the taste for celebration, we passively watch television, also losing touch with our centre.

In l'Arche many of the men and women we welcome have never had a home, or at least a 'happy' home. They had been placed in hospitals or other institutions. They have never experienced the joys and warmth of a family. Even if they lived in a family, they have been hurt by rejection and misunderstandings. This inner pain or trauma breaks down something inside them and often prevents normal psychological development. A few, however, find it normal to leave their parents, like their brothers and sisters, to work and live at l'Arche. All of them have a need for 'family life', and even for basics like a comfortable bedroom where they can hang their pictures and posters on the walls. They need their own bed, their own wardrobe and a place for the things that are precious to them.

At the beginning of l'Arche, the local authorities wanted to oblige us to have a communal kitchen for all our homes. The state would finance the construction of small homes if we would have a communal kitchen because, they said, meals would be less expensive. We had to struggle so that each of our houses could have its own kitchen, despite all the inconveniences and the costs. Forty years at l'Arche have confirmed the importance of the family kitchens, and personalised meal-times in each home, for the healing and the growth of people with wounded emotions. This is true for the assistants also. The kitchen and the dining room table are privileged places for friendship, celebration and relaxation (and, contrary to state expectations, meals are less expensive).

If one does not have a home, one feels the pangs of loneliness, and runs the risk of becoming aggressive or depressed. The heart is not at rest. One becomes hyperactive, running frantically all over the place, seeking distractions, unable to listen, without inner peace. One runs the risk of destroying oneself and others.

Those who put most of their energies into work, overdevelop their aggressive qualities and do not give enough time to family, community, and the spirit of welcome. Their hearts are in danger of atrophy. This lack of balance in their lives will affect their sexuality.

Home, however, is not always a particular place. I know a woman who lives alone and whose work demands much travel. One day she said to me: 'I am like a snail. I carry my home on my back.' Some people are comfortable with themselves. They have found a meaning to their lives, and a certain wholeness or inner unity. They have their friends and people they can turn to. They don't need another 'house'. I believe that this woman had also found that God is her home and that she herself is the home of God.

Family or community life is the special place in which we come to know ourselves in truth. In political and social struggles, the enemy is always outside ourselves. We can identify who and where the enemy is. We want to be victorious and believe we are right, the elite. In family and community life, however, we quickly discover that the enemy is within us, preventing us from being open and able to share. It is the enemy within who incites us to jealousy, infidelity, egotistical attitudes and blockages. To live in a family or in community is always humiliating for our ego which prefers to excel. We quickly discover our darkness and faults, as well as how much we need to grow and to be forgiven.

Thus, the home complements the world of work and social activity. It is the place where one can live committed relationships. It is essential for growth towards wholeness.

The Challenge of L'Arche

For a l'Arche house to become truly 'home', it is necessary that not only those with an intellectual disability put down roots, but that the assistants do as well. If the assistants are always changing, they will never really develop bonds with the core members, and true community will fail to develop. There will not be 'a family'.

At l'Arche, it is not only a question of living with people who have a disability, but of living with them *as family*. This includes giving them the chance to voice their opinions and to participate in decisions. It is a question of sharing our lives with them, not according to a hierarchy of power, but in a community, a 'body' where each one truly has a place.

This is the challenge of l'Arche. There will always be those with intellectual disabilities who are in need. Will there be those who are ready to live with them as in a family? To live with an anguished man or woman whose emotional life is shattered can create or awaken anguish in the assistants, who then come to discover their own limits and wounds. Some residences and centres began by welcoming people in deep distress and without family. They started with the hope of living a full community life together, but little by little they have become institutionalised. The staff, who initially lived as a family with those they had welcomed, gradually reduced the time which they spent in the residence. 'It is just not possible to live together,' they say. They have been 'burnt-out' by the tensions, the lack of support, and spiritual and intellectual impoverishment. Will l'Arche succumb to the same fate? Will we be able to find the necessary formation, resources and life-style which will allow assistants to put down their roots in the community and live together with men and women who have suffered rejection?

Many people with learning disabilities in l'Arche do gradually become rooted. If they come from a family where they were well accepted, they will, perhaps, have difficulty in putting down their roots with us, as they may still long to be with their parents. Sometimes, too, their parents, even though they are happy to have found a solution for their son or daughter, have difficulty accepting that they have found a real home in l'Arche. One cannot have two homes. I know a young woman with a disability who lived from Monday to Friday in a residence (not a l'Arche home); she also had her own flat, and went quite frequently to live with her father. Such dispersion challenges rootedness. In order to grow humanly, there must be one special place for the heart and the emotional life. If there are several places, there will be a lack of unity, which is not conducive to growth towards wholeness.

Home implies a personal choice. Many who come to l'Arche do not have this choice. They are placed with us by their parents or a social worker. It takes time for them to find a certain peace and unity in their being and to discover who they are and what they want to do with their lives. After a few years, it is important for them to be able to choose to stay in the original home, go on to another, or even to leave to live independently if that is possible and what they want. This implies the need for a number of homes or apartments in a community and the possibility of living elsewhere so that each person can, if possible, *choose* his or her own home. I began the first l'Arche home with two men in 1964. By 1966 eight men had been welcomed into the home. Eleven years later six of the eight men had chosen to live in another l'Arche home and the seventh was living independently.

Sexual Difficulties When One Has No 'Home'

Children who are born into a loving family have an 'earth' into which they can put down roots. They know their origins and they know they are loved. Family is the place where they grow and their hearts flourish. However, they may discover that this home is too small for them. They need to leave in order to grow and to discover the world. They leave to find work, and to partake in social and religious activities which open them to broader horizons. They leave to find companionship and to find their place in the world. To begin with, they might live alone in a small flat until one day they feel called to found their own family.

Thus a new family and a new home is founded, a place of rest for the heart, a place of tenderness, of celebration and of forgiveness. It is a place which can become the springboard for other activities elsewhere. The love and peace of the heart which is experienced at home must be spread further. One works not only to earn money but to help other men and women to live in dignity and peace, to have their own 'home' which will be a source of life and a place of renewal.

I have noticed that some people who are quite immature do not want a home or do not think that a home is necessary. They are not yet ready to enter into true relationship and share their life with another. Nor are they ready for all the responsibilities that come with commitment. They like to meet others in bars or other leisure places, but they don't want to stop, rest, or be at home in their bodies. Sometimes there is so much anguish in them that they can be searching without knowing what they are looking for. They can develop sexual disorders which are difficult to overcome. I remember a single man who told me about his terrible need to masturbate. He often decided to stop, but the more he struggled, the more disturbed and tense he became. Finally it was impossible for him to keep his resolution and he fell into terrible guilt feelings. Masturbation became a means by which he relieved tension. It was a vicious circle. In speaking with him, I discovered he led a hyperactive life without any leisure or time for real relaxation. He was on the go from morning to night. He had friends at work, but he did not have a home in the real sense of the word. Nor did he have friends with whom he could relax. I suggested that he try to find a more harmonious and human life-style, one with less stress and with times where he could invite friends to his home, eat with them, waste time with them. This would perhaps ease some of his anguish. When we ignore our heart, sexual drives tend to mount to the surface to remind us that we are not disembodied spirits. This is not to deny that the fundamental problem is the anguish and guilt which were at the root of his hyperactivity.

I am uneasy when I see how some priests live. Their house is like a hotel, a place where they sleep and where they work. It is not a home, a place of relaxation, of welcome, of rest and prayer. They are hyperactive men who run about doing all sorts of things, but they don't seem to have any anchor. Their whole being constantly cries out their need for a place of repose and celebration. Of course, for consecrated men and women their place of repose could be prayer – long moments spent with Jesus, in communion with him. In order to live this life of prayer, we need fellowship, a community full of warmth and tenderness. If we have neither fellowship nor communion with God, the heart runs the risk of hardening itself or exploding in anguish. Both the human body and the human heart have exacting laws which must be respected. All human beings have need of a family, of a home, where life is good.

If so many people with learning disabilities have emotional and sexual difficulties, it is often because they feel ill at ease in their homes and, even more so, in institutions or large residences. In order to integrate our sexual instincts, we need the tenderness of friends, of a family or of a community.

In 1981 I attended a congress in Lyon on 'Handicap and Sexuality'. I was saddened when a staff member of a large Canadian hospital with 600 beds for people with severe disabilities explained how he sought to initiate his adolescents and his young adults into an active sexual life. He taught them to touch one another. To me, it was so evident that this was not what the young people needed. They did not need a hospital – where they felt necessarily anonymous and abandoned – but a family, or a new family, who would become a welcoming and compassionate home. These young people obviously experience feelings of rejection and live in anguish. They need a substitute father or mother, who will touch their bodies with tenderness, who will welcome them, confirm them, and who will recognise their value. They need brothers and sisters, friends and companions. Having been deprived of a warm milieu and of loving and permanent relationships with their parents or with another adult, their bodies cry out to be touched. It is necessary for the staff of that hospital to respond to their cries, giving them friendship and tenderness. Their need is for people who are committed to them.

Alas family is often not the adequate place for some adults with intellectual disabilities who may be given the impression of being a disturbance for the family. They cannot find their place. They know that their brothers and sisters are admired for their progress in school or at work and they see them leaving home to get married. They get the impression that they are hindrances. Despite all the efforts of the parents, it is difficult for those with disabilities to integrate themselves into the normal family rhythm. There are so many things that they cannot share. Conversations are quick and often too intellectual, and no one has time to explain. Visitors may not adjust to the slower rhythm they need.

When people are not part of a family and, above all, when they live isolated lives because of a broken self-image, they live loneliness and anguish. This is one of the most terrible of human sufferings. It becomes imperative for the person to find compensations which will calm this interior turmoil and bring a feeling of well-being, if only for a few minutes.

Escape from anguish can be sought through work, projects, alcohol, drugs, in hyperactivity or in various kinds of sexual relationships. All these compensations however are never able to fill the heart. After a moment of excitement they leave the person even more lonely and in deeper anguish. They increase the sense of isolation.

When we are not living in a loving environment, we can harbour doubts about our essential worth, our value as a person, and live in anguish. There is a fear of being our self, or revealing our true self for fear of a new rejection. There is the constantly nagging question: 'Is it possible that someone can love me for myself, or do I always have to appear interesting, seductive, capable and rich? At first, I can seduce you and you will come near to me. However, later, in living with me you will discover who I am and then reject me.'

This is the terrible cycle which often ends in despair. Is it possible that the day will come when we will discover faithful friends who accept us just as we are, with our fragilities and our gifts? It is then that we will come to accept ourselves as we are, we will let down the barriers which we have built around our fears and vulnerabilities. Then we can live a bonding, a covenant, a commitment with others.

A Sense of Belonging

Like all of us, the first thing that someone with disabilities needs is to feel at home. It is the sense of belonging to a group and of finding one's place there. Belonging, as Abraham Maslow tells us, is a fundamental element in the realisation of the self. Someone who feels they are a burden on others, or feels welcomed only out of pity, cannot feel at home. This is why those with disabilities often need to leave their family and to live in a residence better organised and structured to meet their needs, and with a rhythm of life adapted to them. Then they can grow to greater freedom and make choices. Some will find a community where they feel truly at home, where they are loved and respected and where they have a special role and responsibility. They will progress in the integration of their beings and in their human and spiritual development and the pacification of chaotic sexual urges.

In some centres, men and women with intellectual disabilities are encouraged to have sexual relations with others and exert 'the right' to sexual pleasure without any demands of a true or lasting relationship with the other person. This separation of sexual activity from its connection with the heart reduces the value, spiritual and human, of the sexual act, and creates a separation within the person between the body and the heart, preventing the person from becoming more fully human. Sexual relations do not spring then from a deep friendship, and quickly fall into unhealthy habits which can turn into harmful separations. This encouragement on the part of the staff can be an escape from the demands of presence to people with disabilities who need, above all, to have their own home, integrated in a small town or neighbourhood.

Community life, with its celebrations, its sharings and its love, gives a sense of belonging and security. I remember when l'Arche bought a new home in the village of Trosly. I met Simon on the street. He is a man with a profound disability. He said to me, 'I hear we bought the house on the Square.' He did not say, 'L'Arche bought ...' or 'You bought ...' but 'We bought ...' That 'We' is significant. Simon has the sense of belonging in l'Arche; he has found a new family.

When one feels a sense of belonging to a group, it is easier to espouse its values. Community life is not a hotel where temporary sexual encounters may occur. It implies common values, including those values related to the expressions of love. Community life implies clear options: one is either married or single. If one is single, one does not live as a couple; one lives only as brother and sister. The period of engagement or courtship for a man and a woman in the community who are moving towards marriage – whether they be assistants or those with disabilities – is not easy because they are between two situations. They may be sharing life in the same household, but are not yet married nor are they are really single.

Community relationships resemble the relationship which exists between brothers and sisters in a family. These are simple, deep relationships, full of affection, where each complements and respects the difference of the other, and exclude any sexual relationship.

This matter becomes delicate when there are people in a community who refuse to adhere to the values of the community. They reject this aspect of belonging and want to form a couple outside the bonds of marriage, implying impermanence and in-stability. In such cases, there will be a threat to the foundations of the whole community life, destroying the dynamics of a group based on fraternity.

The Refusal to Belong

At l'Arche, experience has shown us that community life responds to the needs of the vast majority of people with real intellectual disabilities. However, there are some who cannot accept this kind of belonging. There are too many people in the home, and too many demands. They need more personal time and space. They want greater freedom; to live alone. If not everyone is able to live in community situations, everyone needs to belong somewhere in this world. For this reason at l'Arche we must offer living situations that permit people to belong to the community, and also to have the personal space that they need. The danger for some is to fall into an 'adolescent' group that becomes like a gang.

There are those who come from hospitals or from their own families, for whom community life with its slower rhythm, the place it gives to each one, and its celebrations, seems too wonderful. It cannot be for them. They are too broken. They feel too guilty and too angry, convinced that no one is able to love them because they are too 'bad and ugly'. They need time to test love, to discover that it is possible to be loved, that the community is truly theirs.

There are those who are too greatly shattered and whose defences are too strong. Community life with its tenderness, its celebrations, and its fraternal relationships with those of the other sex, can put them in difficulty. It awakens old wounds and can become a place of anguish and pain, manifested through behaviour which shows that they do not want to belong to the group. It is necessary for them to leave, though they may not always know how to say this or to show it. Often they can be violent or anti-social, hoping to ensure that they will be sent away. Some refuse to be in l'Arche, because they cannot stand being separated from their parents. They refuse to have confidence in others because this would imply an acceptance of their situation away from Mum and Dad.

Finally, there are those who, strictly speaking, do not have a serious deficiency on the intellectual level. They are in l'Arche simply because there was no other more appropriate institution to welcome them. They suffer from a lack of education, of family support and of self esteem. They have been classified as disabled more or less by mistake, and excluded from other avenues of welcome and education. Some of these people are able to accept the community in the hope that it will be a springboard to go further. Others refuse it because they cannot accept being identified with those having more serious disabilities. In various ways they show their disagreement and desire to leave.

With the help of professionals from outside, the community must try to decode these different refusals to belong. The 'no' may be a sign of a deeper 'yes'. It may also say: 'If you truly want to love me, come and look for me.' The 'no' may say, 'I cannot bear this life; it is too dangerous for me', or: 'This life is good, but I do not have any disability. I am capable of living my life on my own, with the friends of my choice and of one day founding my own family. You must recognise this and help me to go further.'

I remember Greg. From the moment of his arrival at l'Arche, and for many years after, he refused all community services. He hid in his room or went outdoors alone. Fortunately, the person responsible for the home did not force him to do the dishes or participate in community events. Actually, Greg was not really deficient on an intellectual level; he was epileptic, and his divorced parents could no longer keep him. They placed him in an institution which sent him to the psychiatric hospital because of his crises of violence. These were messages which the institution did not know how to decode. Greg had a negative image of himself. He wondered whether he was sick, violent or crazy. In fact, none of these images corresponded to the reality. Greg was a victim of injustice and incompetence in the educational sphere. His refusal to belong to the group was a healthy sign. He was indicating his desire and capacity to be independent. Today, Greg works as a plumber. He is still a little unsociable. He lives in a small house with another man who has been along a similar road, and they are entirely responsible for themselves.

John-Paul had had a similar background, but his refusal to belong was less clear. He would say, 'Yes, I will do this or that' out of fear of causing pain, but then he would not do it; he had 'forgotten'. John-Paul is gentle and the image he has of himself is certainly less negative. Later, he too left l'Arche to live in an apartment. Several years ago he found competitive employment. Last year he married.

The Great Need of the Human Heart

One of the greatest questions in each one of us is: 'Am I of value? Is there someone who believes enough in me to be concerned about me and to live a covenant relationship with me?' This cry for bonds of friendship and recognition is lived out in different ways.

There is the cry to be loved by a father and mother who will hold one in one's weakness. It is a cry which springs from the fragility of the infant or the insecurity of the adolescent. It is the cry of the adult with a learning disability who needs tenderness, welcome, kindness, compassion, personal nourishment, support and encouragement. It is a cry which says: 'I need you. Your love gives me life and roots.' It is the cry of every human person, because each one of us carries our fragilities and our difficulties. Each of us cries out to be loved by someone who will give us support. It is also the cry which turns us to God.

There is also the cry for a friend, an equal, a brother, a sister. One is no longer crying out for a parental figure. This yearning for friendship may become a search for the unique friend in love and marriage.

There is also the deep call to serve and be a friend and companion to the weakest and the poorest. Many of our core members love being a special, compassionate friend to others in the community who have a more severe disability.

In fact, these three cries of the human heart are at the origins of the different types of relationships between people, and are linked together. They are often present, but in different proportions. A break in one of these covenants can affect the others. These relationships constitute the network of affections in which each of us lives and grows. They are the milieu of life which keeps us from falling into isolation.

In order for a home to be truly 'home', it is good that these different kinds of relationships be found there. In our community on the Ivory Coast, Seydou was the first person to be welcomed.

He was 50 years old, a Muslim from Niger. This man of great sensitivity and kindness, had been placed in a psychiatric centre because of depression caused by several earlier misfortunes in his life. He died several years later, killed by a truck as he walked home one night. Soon after Seydou had been welcomed into the community, we also welcomed a few children with disabilities. The presence of different ages brought something deeply human into the community. A community often needs grandparents and grandchildren. The mixture of different ages, strengths and weaknesses, gifts and individual qualities gives harmony to a family. There is a special peace and a balance to the emotional life of each one. These differences allow each person to find a particular role, helping one another to live more fully.

The Home Can Stifle

The home, and the family living there, are the soil in which children find life and security. It is there that they are formed. Their lives are centred around their parents, who protect and educate them. Little by little, as they grow and develop, they find their centre within themselves and are able to leave their parents, to join with another and to give new life, founding another family, another home.

Between the moment when one lives with one's parents and the time when one creates a new family with another, there is a very rich period of adolescence. Young people search, becoming conscious of their bodies, their strengths and abilities, but also of their fears and weaknesses.

During adolescence one lives at home, but it seems too confining. There is the risk of being smothered there. So, the individual puts one foot (and sometimes two) outside the home. It can be rather agonising, like being between two chairs.

What does this mean for people who have a disability? Of course, it is good that they have a place for the heart and where they can put down roots. But they too must not be smothered there. It is not easy to find a balance between roots and fruits, between security and insecurity, between the comfort of home and the fear of growing.

They may live in a residence, which is not a community but resembles a boarding house or a hotel. The rules can be too rigid, so they seek refuge elsewhere, perhaps in the home of a companion or in sexual encounters. If the community is too warm and affectionate and does not leave enough space for personal growth, then the person runs the risk of being stifled and of losing some of their vitality and need for risk. A community can give life, but it can also hinder it. This is why a home welcoming people with learning disabilities should be open to neighbours, friends, new assistants and visitors. There is a great danger if it closes in on itself. It is necessary that those who live there have more and more friends from outside who visit them. The community needs to be a home, a place of tenderness and security, but also a place which is a springboard or an oasis of nourishment enabling those who can, to go on to a new stage in life.

Chapter Five

THE COMMUNITY: PLACE OF SEXUAL INTEGRATION

Many of those who come to l'Arche from institutions have suffered in their bodies and their hearts. They have been neither accepted nor loved for and in themselves. In their fragility and anguish they are often unable to either accept or love themselves. Hidden within is a profound, and sometimes violent, anger which they are not able to control. The first stage at l'Arche is generally a time of putting down roots, finding peace and a sense of belonging. This time of healing can sometimes be long. It requires authentic relationships in a warm familial community and also work, which gives people a sense of their dignity and reveals capabilities which had been latent in them. In this way they can begin to break out of the vicious circle of being closed up in themselves and discover others, with their joys, pains and needs. They begin to be able to open up, and to live, and share with others in community.

Today many people with less severe learning disabilities are coming to l'Arche. They have often been to specialised schools for adolescents and have developed in a more harmonious way psychologically and socially. Some do not want to live in a community setting with many others. They do not feel the need for the structures, which seem to them too confining. They perceive the structures of community as taking away their freedom, rather than giving security. They just want to live independently and have a boy or girl friend. They are very influenced by what the media proposes, by the lives of other young people today, and by the way they want to live their sexuality. When and if they find themselves in l'Arche, community life for them can often be a place of transition which can help them move from immaturity to greater maturity. For this to occur, they need to be well accompanied.

The ability to really become a part of a community implies that the person is willing to gradually make the transition from 'the others for me' to 'me for the others'. The decision to accept others as persons who are important and to take on a bit of responsibility for others is a fundamental choice which all human beings are called to make. This choice needs to be accompanied by continuing efforts to grow beyond the selfishness and the world of darkness and fear, which are in each one of us.

Many in l'Arche have made this transition from being closed in on themselves to openness and life. When Vivian came to our community in Honduras, she was like a wild girl. She was ten years old, blind and autistic, and had spent nearly all her life in an asylum. She had never experienced any permanent relationship. In the asylum, which was a difficult place, she had been able to survive only with a lot of pain. Coming to us she experienced more pain to begin with. At l'Arche she was with 'strangers' and became even more insecure and more anguished. She screamed continuously. She ate her clothes and smeared the walls with her excrement. She severely tested the team of assistants who, by their love, their unity, and by the grace of God, were able to respond to her insecurity. Gradually, over many months, she discovered she was loved and she began to feel secure. She remains fragile and still has trouble with relationships, but there is a peace in her face and body, a sign of the resurrection of her heart.

Many in l'Arche however, have not been able to make such a spectacular transition. They continue to carry their psychological disorders, their anger and their frustrations, which have their origins in childhood, and which they are often not able to express. Such people have not really changed, though perhaps they have begun to move toward a sense of sharing, or have found a certain dignity in work. In some sense, the community has become their home. However, their wounds are deep, and they continue to live in suffering and instability.

Dreams of Marriage

It is not surprising that many of these people seek a refuge in dreams. The greater the wounds, the more they need their dreams, especially when the community is not able to respond to all their needs. A community is never perfect; it is a very human reality: this naturally implies weakness and fragility. Some of those with disabilities will be dissatisfied, even angry, with the community, which, because of its own inadequacies and because of the depths of some peoples' wounds, is unable to respond to their cries. Thus, they dream of an ideal place, a place of rest where they will be totally loved and where they will be the centre of attention. They dream of perfect happiness.

Peter had encephalitis when he was a child; it left him with one good leg and one good arm; he has a real intellectual disability as well. He compensates for his physical disabilities by a flood of words. He dreams of being a radio commentator. When someone feels impoverished, diminished, they tend to flee into the imagination. How do we make a link between an intolerable reality and an inaccessible dream, between the loneliness in reality, and the loneliness in the dream?

Claude is very much at home in l'Arche and appreciates its values, but he is still sensitive to the desires of his mother. Sometimes his mother and l'Arche are in conflict over decisions as to where he will spend his holiday, or questions related to his health or his diet. It is not easy for Claude, caught between two very real authorities in his life. How can he escape? He is forced sometimes to escape into dreams, where, in some way, he can be himself, away from the conflicts.

It is important to see the different roles dreams can play. The dream may, in some cases, open someone to reality and love; in others, it may cut someone off from reality.

Dreams or fantasies can be particularly strong, in order to excite sexuality or to masturbate. People can withdraw into the 'virtual', imagining that they are in a relationship of love and of sexuality. This, like drugs or alcohol, can produce momentary enjoyment, imagining that they are no longer in the anguish of loneliness. Living these moments of fantasy can become an addiction and, like drugs, can render even more difficult a true relationship where the person is called to be sensitive to the real, not imaginary, needs of the other. It is healthy to dream. It shows that life is stronger than death, that there is hope within us. Not to dream can be a sign of utter despair. Dreams, like psychosis, are a refusal of death; a way of reacting to inner pain. It is important therefore not to shatter the dreams of others too quickly on the grounds of putting people in touch with reality, a reality which may be unbearable for them. When a physical disability constantly reminds one of one's powerlessness, reality can be unbearable. At the same time, to allow a person to be buried in the world of dreams or drugs can in some way confirm them in isolation. An experience of drugs can give a certain sense of life and excitement, but after the temporary high each one is left terribly alone.

Dreams do not bring happiness, but sometimes they allow someone to live and to survive. We should not disturb people's dreams unless we love them with great tenderness and caution so that they might discover that reality is not hell and that they have a place there.

A great difficulty which confronts people with disabilities today is the image and the myth of marriage in our society and culture. So much publicity is based on the image of the happy couple; the films and magazines so often present that marvellous love which 'brings happiness'. These are the images which a person retains rather than those of the reality of difficulties in building relationships and of the pain of separation and infidelity.

It is not surprising that so many people with disabilities dream of marriage. For most of them, work and the couple are the only models they have for belonging to the adult world. To become an adult, to be free and 'normal', is to marry or to have a partner like one's brothers and sisters. Their own singleness makes them feel inferior.

I remember Frances. She was twenty-three years old when she came to us. She was intelligent but walled up behind psychological barriers. It was a tremendous suffering for her to be separated from her family. Shortly after a weekend visit to them, she refused to eat and became almost immobile. She became bedridden and when the situation worsened she had to go to hospital. Several weeks later, she died. I discovered that during that last weekend with her family, in a crisis of violence, she had thrown the picture frame out of the window in which there was a photo of her younger sister on her wedding day. I think Frances died of grief, despair, and jealousy over her younger sister's happiness, a happiness which seemed to have been denied to her.

Some men and women with intellectual disabilities dream of marriage; they dream of being 'unique' to someone, and of living in intimacy with that person. Their bodies often search for the tenderness that they did not have in their childhood.

To dream of marriage is to dream of being queen or king of the feast, to have one's own home and space in which to live; it is the dream of being in paradise. Is not the wedding feast the great dream of humanity, the sign of the kingdom of Heaven?

When someone speaks of wanting to get married, it is important to interpret exactly what he or she is saying. I asked Peter, for example, what marriage meant to him. He answered: 'Oh, it is to have a wife who will look after me.' For another it might mean: 'I want to be like everyone else. I want to be like my big brother so that my parents no longer look down on me' or 'I want to be loved and seen as someone special'. Or else it could mean 'I no longer want to live in community with lots of other people. I want to have my own home. I need your help to leave this place'.

We must not underestimate the pain of those with disabilities when an assistant marries. I was painfully aware of this when Bernadette married James. Several men in the home were upset, not only because of the marriage, which was a state inaccessible to them, but, above all, because Bernadette whom they loved was leaving them. They were jealous of James; Bernadette preferred to live with James than with them. They suffered from this. Yet, obviously Bernadette needed to live her own life and to follow her own calling. We all suffer when we feel that we have not been chosen. We all have a need to be chosen by someone. This does not mean that we must have an intimate or exclusive relationship. It does mean that we need to have relationships that confirm that we are special and that we are loved.

The pain of people with disabilities is the same pain of so many other people who want to marry, to be loved in a unique way, but who never seem to find the right partner they yearn and hope for. It is the suffering of all those who have separated and are plunged into loneliness.

Community and Culture

People with intellectual disabilities are inevitably influenced by the values and ideas in their immediate surroundings with regard to relationships and sexuality between men and women Similarly they are influenced by the mass media with its concept of love as the source of perfect happiness for couples, and by the often contradictory values of their own families. These have formed their imagination and it is not surprising therefore that they live in a certain amount of confusion.

In fact, the surrounding culture is itself ambivalent. Through it comes the dream of humanity – to be happy, to live in loving relationships; but it also shows the isolation and anguish of those who live for themselves, seeking to fill up the void in their heart by material possessions which lead them to struggle, to compete and often, to be violent. This culture is very seductive. It captures the deepest energies of a human being. At l'Arche, we find people with a compulsive desire to possess things. Community life, on the other hand, based on listening and sharing, is a school for growth in love and communion. This new culture, founded on the Gospel values, is so different to the values of the surrounding culture and all that is shown on television and movie screens.

Despite the powerful seduction of images and publicity, I am amazed by the qualities of goodness which one finds not only in those with learning disabilities, but in each human being. The human heart is fragile, falling easily into the snares of seduction, but it also desperately yearns for authentic love, lived in a bond of tenderness and peace with others. The human heart always recognises the authenticity of true love even if it is sometimes afraid of its demands.

The illusions projected by the mass media and publicity can leave an emptiness in the heart. They do not ease anguish and the fear of isolation, but can augment them. They arouse, but are not able to satisfy, the heart thirsting for presence, creativity, communion, and infinity.

L'Arche, like other communities and many families, wishes to respond to this most fundamental need of human beings. It wants to be a place of authentic relationships which flower in celebrations of joy, where each one can find the deepest meaning of life and touch the goodness and the beauty of his or her personality. It wishes to help each one to live the bonds of unity in a depth of love where all, especially the weakest ones, may find their place and carry a certain responsibility for themselves and others.

But, l'Arche is not a ghetto, or a 'hothouse' cut off from the world. The surrounding culture has formed the conscious, and often the unconscious, world of each one of us. This culture has pervaded each one of us, and through us, the community. This forces us to clarify the direction in which we orient our lives. At the same time, it may increase certain sufferings, keeping certain wounds open. Those who are frail and anguished have need of structures and solid references which our modern world rarely provides. On the contrary, it often augments anguish, isolation, fear and lack of trust in one another.

A sixteen-year-old girl said to me: 'Plays, films, novels and different forms of art awaken deep aspects of my being which real life does not awaken.' The daily routine of school and family life seemed boring to her compared with the deep emotions and sense of life she felt through art. How to help someone like her to discover not only the need to blossom in her personhood, but also to become more mature in relationships and to accept that those deep emotions can by-pass responsibility. Real life and real responsibility can bring risk and adventure.

The challenge of community life is precisely to offer an alternative which responds to the deepest human aspirations of belonging. Such an alternative, however, is not possible without a certain inner struggle. 'The truth shall make you free,' Jesus said. Yet, we are afraid of the truth and the responsibilities which liberty brings. This is the challenge of all education. Nevertheless, our experience of community has shown that the values by which we try to live have truly helped men and women to grow in their inner selves, to find meaning, direction and hope in their lives.

Interpreting Behaviour

'The Angel and the Beast'[1] is a booklet on the findings of parents and educators on the sexuality of people with intellectual disabilities. It is the result of a study of sheltered workshops and group homes in Paris and its suburbs. The first part shows the naivety of parents who are not able, or who refuse, to look at the sexual needs of their children. The second part of the book shows how educators focus on the genital sexuality of men and women with a disability. The title of the book, 'The Angel and the Beast', is revealing. It is so easy to deny genital sexuality or, on the other hand, to separate it from the totality of a person's being and their most fundamental needs.

Educators are called to look at the totality of each person, their wholeness, seeking the meaning of their cry. When someone is violent, that violence is a cry, an expression, a form of communication. We must try not only to stop the violence and pacify the person, but also to understand what the violence is saying and decipher the message it contains.

In l'Arche, as we learn to interpret acts of violence, we are discovering that they can be a cry for attention, a cry of revolt against an injustice or frustration, or a cry coming from a suffering in childhood that has been awoken. This cry is more frequent in homes where there is little celebration and animation and where personal relationships of communion can be missing. This violence can in fact be provoked by assistants when they are not really present or creative. Perhaps they are tired, or tied up in their own problems or tensions. In such cases, it is not so much the people with disabilities who need to change, but the assistants. This can be difficult for them to accept. They, too, have the right to be themselves with their wounds and their sufferings. Of course, the person with disabilities who has been violent must change too. Violence is not an appropriate response to a lack of attention, and all of us must learn to live with a certain level of frustration.

Not long ago, Richard had been reprimanded unjustly. He was furious. He went to his room and tore up three ten euros notes. Talking with me later, he said: 'Three years ago, I would have been violent, now I just tear up money.' This was a progress, especially because he was able to verbalise it afterwards. But the assistant who reprimanded him unjustly must change too.

When Simon becomes violent, it is often because he has received a message from his father: 'Do not come home this weekend.' Simon suffers from this, all the more so because his father now lives with a new wife, and this has thrown Simon into confusion. It is more difficult for him to contain his emotions and to channel his anguish. He is more fragile than Richard and needs more attention from the assistants.

It is equally important to decipher the gestures of genital sexuality. 'The Angel and the Beast' shows how the subject of genital sexuality is an area of conflict within institutions, and between institutions and parents.[2] This is inevitable, because of different values and because of the personal sufferings and sense of guilt within both parties. Genital sexuality becomes the focus of the conflict. The authors show how attitudes towards genital sexuality are ambivalent and often carry a double message.

Permissiveness is held up as the ideal by many educators, but such advocates of permissiveness always speak in general terms which are rarely practised in specific and complex situations. To exercise restraint on those with disabilities is seen as repressive, yet these same educators argue the need for restraint in response to social convention and the compulsive sexuality of some people with learning disabilities.

In their article, 'Needs that are not recognised',[3] Dr Stanislas Tomkiewicz and Dr Elizabeth Zucman speak of the opposing views of some specialists and parents. The former place less emphasis on the emotional needs of people with disabilities and more on the genital sexual needs which are seen by them to be stronger than those of many young people. They even describe their sexual urges as being rather bestial. For the authors, there seems to be a contradiction between the permissive ideology of the specialists and their rather deprecating attitude to the sexuality of people with disabilities. The authors then go on to point out the confusion this attitude causes in those who have a disability, especially if it is slight. One the one hand, they are told to practise moderation, to control their sexual activities; and, on the other hand, they are given contraceptive devices which seem to indicate permission, if not encouragement, to a freer sexual expression.[4]

It is important to interpret the sexual and violent acts of people with disabilities in residences or institutions. What exactly is the person saying or wanting when he or she seeks a sexual relationship in this specific place? The person knows that these acts are not 'inoffensive' and 'neutral' and can provoke all sorts of strong reactions from the staff, and sometimes even conflict between staff members. Certainly the person may be governed by a sexual urge or a yearning for closeness to someone of the other sex, but he or she can also take delight in the strong reactions and conflicts which he or she has provoked.

In the same way, it is important to understand what a Down's syndrome lady of twenty-one is really trying to say when she declares that she wants to go to bed with a man, especially if she is terribly unhappy in her family, or has no relationships in her life in which she is special and unique. No serious psychologist who has any real contact with human beings can say that sexual desire is simply an urge which *must* be satisfied. We mentioned earlier three situations which illustrate the complexity of apparently sexual behaviour:[5] Edith, who uses her charm to attract men,

Micheline, who has captivated Bernard, and Francis who is influenced by the image his mother has of him. It seems that in none of these situations are the people really looking for sexual pleasure as such, and certainly not for real relationships. Edith is seeking the pleasure of being noticed and of making men jealous of her; Micheline, the pleasure of having Bernard on a leash, giving her a sense of power; and Francis, the pleasure of living up to his mother's image of him.

There are young people who use drugs in a desire to disgrace their fathers. In an underhand way, they are seeking revenge for their father's lack of love, of attention and tenderness. We cannot deny the variety of underlying motivations in behaviour.

Jeremy is a big, gentle lad who suffers from a psychosis. He has great difficulties with language and relationships. He is attracted to the young girls who visit the community and to the beauty of their bodies. Gently, he approaches them to touch them. There is something beautiful in this attraction, but on the other hand, Jeremy cannot respond to the deep needs of these young girls. He can neither understand their call for friendship, nor their fear of him. He is incapable of being a support to them, or of feeling responsible for them. This attraction will not help him to develop true friendship in which the boundaries are clear and differences are respected. To permit or encourage Jeremy in a physical union with a woman would be to encourage him into a union which is only 'fusional'. It would not help him to become more deeply human.

The role of the educator is to help those with a disability to live humanly and this could include having sexual relationships when they can really be human and not divorced from their lives or from their most fundamental and personal needs. The educator's role is to help someone with a disability not simply to express each violent or sexual urge, but to integrate these instincts in a true and permanent relationship.

The sexual drive in the human being cannot be separated from the deep need for relationship if it is to remain truly human. It can be a cry for momentary pleasure or it can be a need to be liberated from the sexual urge. Often the sexual urge erupts when someone feels alone and anguished. It then seeks expression on the level of genital sexuality. But more deeply, the person can be crying out for a friendship which he cannot live because of his fear of relationship. We yearn to be loved, but at the same time we are frightened of it because it makes us vulnerable. Sometimes it can be easier for a girl to believe that her body is desirable than to believe her person is lovable. Some people with intellectual disabilities do not believe either in the beauty of their person or in their capacity to love profoundly and to be loved. They are judged so frequently on purely exterior criteria of normality and abnormality; how can they believe that their person is lovable and that they are important just as they are? To reduce genital sexuality to being only a liberation of a passing external urge without attaching it to life and fecundity, is to diminish the person.

It is important to interpret acts of genital sexuality wisely in order to understand the most profound needs of the person and to help each one to move towards fulfilment.

Integration of Sexuality

At l'Arche, it is evident to us that the most essential thing for human beings is to have deep relationships of friendship. In 'The Angel and the Beast' the authors show a discrepancy between the vision of some parents and that of certain educators. Parents feel their children seek affection above all, while educators think that they search primarily for sexual pleasure.

Don't we need to go beyond these two attitudes? Of course, expressions of 'love' on the part of those having intellectual disabilities are often very affectionate. In my opinion, however, what they seek is much more than a passing emotion or a feeling of affection. They, as all of us, want to be linked to people, entering into a true friendship which involves fidelity. The signs of 'innocent' affection or of 'genital sexuality' are two aspects of the same call, the same cry: 'Do you truly love me and respect me? Do you truly wish to commit yourself to me? Is there really a meaning to my life? Do I really have a place in your heart and in the human community?' So many never receive any answer to these questions. They will continue to cry and never discover their true inner selves. They will continue to provoke their parents and teachers, or simply yield to their wishes.

The goal of education is to help people grow toward wholeness and to discover their place, and eventually exercise their gifts, in a network of friendship and, ideally, in an acknowledged convenant relationship. This means the integration of one's sexuality in a vision of fellowship and friendship. It implies that each one, man or woman, in his or her sexual being, is called to discover that they are appreciated and loved. They need to learn to love others, entering into relationships of communion, gift, tenderness and service. The integration of sexuality means that one is no longer ruled by sexual compulsions and the selfish search for pleasure, using others for self. Rather, it is a matter of being faithful to relationships with other people.

John Paul II wrote:

> The experience of certain Christian communities has shown that an intense and stimulating community life, continuous and discreet educational support, the fostering of friendly contacts with properly trained people, the habit of channelling instincts and developing a healthy sense of modesty as respect for their own personal privacy, often succeeds in restoring the emotional balance of persons with mental disabilities and can lead them to live enriching, fruitful and satisfying interpersonal relationships. To show disabled persons that we love them means showing them that we value them. Attentive listening, understanding their needs, sharing their suffering, patience in guidance, are some of the ways to introduce the disabled into a human relationship of communion, to enable them to perceive their own value and make them aware of their capacity for receiving and giving love.[6]

Such an integration of sexuality is never simple. Sexual urges and desires are strong and can drive a person to intercourse without first passing through the different stages of friendship, commitment and communion. So-called 'love' can be seductive and manipulative. It can use others as objects and it can be a way to wield power over them. Sexual urges can also be destructive and linked to aggression and violence.

Nevertheless, in the same sexual urge, there is something very beautiful which in some ways renders its integration difficult. There can be a deep attraction towards another and a desire for intimacy with the person. There is also the desire to give life to a child. It is important to understand the sexual instinct in its complexity, and in some way to dialogue with it. It cannot be smothered or mastered by will power. It must be integrated, little by little, into a true friendship with another and expressed only in the conditions of a real covenant blessed by God.

For me, the integration of genital sexuality is different from the sublimation of the sexual instincts of which the followers of Freud speak so often. Sublimation is seen as the orientation of sexual energies into other creative, intellectual or artistic activities. This of course can be good, but in this a person's pleasure remains the main concern while the importance of relationship with others can be neglected. The integration of sexuality, on the other hand, is assumed in a work of love and communion where one seeks the good certainly for oneself but in a special way for the other. This integration is in and through a relationship with person as a *person*. The life-giving, vital energy – through works of goodness, truth, service and tenderness – is gratified by the loving responses that these gestures call forth.

A True Community

In reality, we cannot dissociate the human sexual urge from the attraction of love. The folly of the sexual urge is in some sense linked to the folly of love, with its search for intimacy, tenderness and true communion. The important thing is to move away from fantasies and illusions of intimacy in the imagination and towards a true love expressed in the reality of communion and gift, and founded on a covenant of commitment. This, in fact, is one of the goals of community. Community is a place of healing and therapy, a place of growth and education for each person; it is a place where each one can live authentic and liberating relationships.

The first priority is to help those with a disability to discover that they are loved with tenderness and care, experienced through the body and in the totality of their being. Through dialogue they are encouraged to grow to greater autonomy. For this, someone must take up the role of education and relationship that was carried by the parents and the family. Thus is born, little by little, a sense of being part of a new family. Then each one will grow to the discovery that they too are capable of loving, of working, of developing their gifts, of serving and living with others as sisters and brothers, of growing to greater autonomy, having personal projects and making choices. In discovering their humanity, they discover the harmony of giving and receiving. Moreover, each discovers also that he or she is a child of God, capable of knowing the Lord of the universe who is also Father. Gradually, each one accepts the relativity of his or her disability and understands that the most important thing is the heart, that which is capable of loving and serving in openness to God and to others. There is less fear of meeting the world because of the links of friendship, and the sense of belonging to something greater than one's family and one's community. Each one is a person who belongs to all human-ity, to the Church and to God, finding the deepest meaning of life in living for others.

A community will only be able to fulfil this role if it is truly community, and not just a group of individuals living in their own way without any sense of a common bond between them. True community is a place of covenant; like a family, its members are linked to one another in mutual trust and respect, and by a deep sense of belonging. This is expressed in the spontaneity and anima-tion of real celebrations and festivities. A family has one soul and one heart. A collection of individuals has neither heart nor soul; it only has rules and a hierarchy of power; in such a situation people can look elsewhere for a life of tenderness and bonds of love. And one of the ways of seeking elsewhere is the cry for genital sexuality, through seduction, obsessions and even perversions.

Community implies a real fellowship where people truly listen to one another in love. In communities like l'Arche, we must try to break down whatever separates those with a disability from those who come to live with them. Sometimes these walls of separation serve to protect assistants from losing their power. Such walls can only be knocked down by love and mutual trust, where the assistants begin to enter into communion with the person who has a disability. Assistants come to serve and to give, but also to receive and to discover their own humanity. Slowly, they can accept the risk of loving, knowing how to make gestures of tenderness and affection in a way that will not awaken genital sexuality, but rather bring fulfilment and peace, and awaken the heart because they are a sign of communion and of covenant.

It is important that this communion be liberating, and not stifling. Affectivity and bonds at the level of the heart are very beautiful realities, but they have their dangers. What often happens in a family can also happen in a community. There can be assistants who, instead of liberating those for whom they are responsible, become controlling or possessive and use them to satisfy their own emotional needs or compulsion for power. They are afraid of loneliness and of separation, and of the aggression that these can imply. They use emotional bonds unconsciously to block growth and to stifle freedom. In communities like those of l'Arche, it is vitally important to guard against this danger.

Only when the bonds of the heart are liberating and not possessive can the community become a place of celebration and vitality, where suffering can be shared and where each one gives life to the other, discovering their unique call and identity.

If we could stop looking at the manifestations of genital sexuality as a right to pleasure or a problem to be solved, and could recognise it more as a cry to create permanent bonds in order to escape isolation and to become more fully human, we would take an enormous step towards understanding true education.

Communities which begin joyfully, in a network of freely offered personal relationships, can become closed in on themselves. This is the story of so many communities which began in the mystery of communion and ended in rules and administration. No community is protected from such danger.

True sexual integration, in the way I have described it, needs a community with a heart and a soul, a sense of belonging and celebration, a fruitfulness, but especially many personal relationships. These conditions can never be guaranteed. Hearts can lose confidence and enthusiasm and barriers can grow up between people.

In some communities of l'Arche, I have occasionally seen signs of lively animation, but closer investigation revealed that some of the core members actually were living in isolation, without either the warmth of real friendship and care or the challenge to growth through personal projects. In sickness they did not experience a special tenderness which is so essential at such times. In situations like this, violence can erupt and the desire for genital sexuality be manifested. These are cries for more attention and love. These same cries are heard whenever a community becomes too autocratic, and those with disabilities do not share enough in the decisions which affect their lives. In brief, violence and the hunger for genital sexuality arise whenever people with disabilities do not feel truly at home.

Chapter Six

SINGLE PEOPLE LIVING IN
COMMUNITY

The Pain of Those Who Are Single

Despite all the human riches we may find in a true community life, it will never totally fill the heart of a person who is single. There will always be a suffering which comes from the absence of a more total intimacy with another and from renouncing physical paternity or maternity. This is true even when one has a privileged friendship with a particular person. There are many reasons that people remain single. Sometimes it is not a choice. Sometimes there is a very clear choice. More total intimacy is renounced because the person is aware of not being able to live fully and in all truth the demands which are necessarily involved in the total gift of one person to another. Sometimes it is a clear choice to be faithful to the desire of God for their lives.

The pain of the single person is real but it can be lived in community in hope, a hope which, in a way assuages the anguish of loneliness. The suffering of those who exercise their genital sexuality without responsibility, commitment, or fecundity is that they are inevitably disappointed. After moments of pleasure, they find themselves in an even greater loneliness: pleasure is so ephemeral and anguish so near!

Marriage also carries its pain. The union is never fully satisfying; it can never be a total union because of the simple fact that the two spouses are always in some sense separate. They are never able to enter certain secret areas of the other; there is never perfect clarity between them, partly because of the fears, the self-centeredness and the shadow areas which still exist in the heart of each one. The honeymoon of love can, over the years and through a lack of communication and attentiveness to one another, turn into a tragedy of conflict. Yet it can also be an exceptional 'school' of learning to love and of understanding more deeply the love of God.

Here we touch the mystery of the human heart, its vulnerability and its thirst for love and presence, its thirst for infinity. The human being is constantly straining towards this infinity: a thirst to be filled, to be recognised in one's uniqueness, a thirst to be free, to be creative and loving, to be a source of life for others. But this pull towards infinity is lived by a fragile being, a being easily seduced by lies or caught up in fears, capable of hate, and seeking power and admiration in what is only illusion. Our thirst is infinite but it is carried in very finite and fragile vessels.

The human heart seems so linked to the sexual organs; and the quest for love is equally linked with the desire to give life. Love, linked in this way to genital sexuality, appears to be the great mystery of the human being. In reality, it is like a marvellous fruit hanging from the tree of life. However, fruit without a tree is an illusion. Love requires inner strength, order and a deep rootedness in the person. It implies that the person is capable of giving to another and, with him or her, of giving to others. It implies faithfulness to the bonds that have been given, especially when a relationship is threatened by moments of difficulty, or when illusion and weakness are exposed.

The thirst for union and fecundity, fruitfulness, in the depths of the human person is in the image of God who is absolute love and infinite fecundity. It is therefore holy, and in order for union and fecundity to be realised in their deepest harmony, the union must receive power and strength from God and be marked by the divine qualities of fidelity and truth. This sacred element in man and woman which draws them to the triune God can be totally degraded when used only for the pursuit of pleasure for self, without any recognition of the value of either fecundity or permanent commitment. Aristotle said that the worst thing is the corruption of the best thing. This is what happens when one loves 'without love', without truly wanting to give oneself to another.

The bonds of love which can exist between a man and a woman are a mystery. The Song of Songs tells of the fire and intimacy of love, a sign of the love of God. The poems of St John of the Cross are songs of love – a passionate love – for the Beloved. Jesus came not to establish reasonable laws which must be obeyed in order that human beings and society function well, but rather to light the fire of the Holy Spirit, to communicate a passion of love which is reflected also in inner light and an outpouring of service. Now this fire of the Holy Spirit is given, not to the wise and the powerful, but to the weak and the smallest ones, to the poor, to the gentle, to the pure of heart and the persecuted. To these Jesus shows himself to be the Beloved.

There will always be discontent in the human heart; it will never be able to live wholly in the land of ecstasy and fulfilment. These are experiences given for a moment but which cannot be permanently contained in the vulnerability of our hearts. Even the most beautiful love ends in separation, for death is written into the human body. In order to welcome that death, or rather, in order to live love fully in mortal bodies, we must have trust: life and love are stronger than death; in spite of separation an invisible union remains, a union which finds its consummation after death, when our mortal bodies will be raised up in glory.

True love is achieved through suffering and sacrifice and doing work on ourselves. It is also a gift. When we love someone, the well-being, liberty, growth, desires or happiness of this person are more precious even than the joy of being with him or her. True love is not possessive, but always liberates. True love is always dynamic and evolving because each person grows and changes; their needs evolve. Possessive love stifles; a love that refuses to accept change and growth can wound the other and may finally destroy the other. Jesus said that there is no greater love than to give one's life for one's friends. Love is consummated in gift of self.

In his first encyclical, 'God is Love', Pope Benedict XVI writes that true love is the meeting of *eros* – which is a passionate and enthusiastic desire for union, communion mutuality and presence with another – and *agape* – which is the desire for the other to be totally fulfilled and which flows from God. The rising *eros* is transformed by the descending love of God. True love is wonderfully human and wonderfully divine. But it implies pain and a real purification of all that is intrinsically 'for self' in the eros so that all is consummated in the gift of self.

Many human beings are obliged to live single.[1] Throughout the history of humanity, men and women have not been able to find the beloved of their hearts. They lived alone, painfully asking themselves if it was because they are unlovable. Many today find themselves in that same situation. For others, the beloved is suddenly torn from them by death. Others enter into the bonds of marriage with the enthusiasm of passionate love, but without the human means for living and deepening the relationship, which eventually breaks down. Then, there are all those who carry severe physical disabilities; others have a fear of relationship, or they had violent or depressive characters or behaviour disorders and were unable to live a harmonious relationship with another. Others with learning disabilities felt rejected and devalued for so many different reasons; they were unable to live a union of love in their flesh. Yet, our experience shows us that when such people live not alone but in community, or in a network of friendship, strengthened and healed by a love which comes from God, it is possible for them to find fulfilment in a life of celibacy.

In the Absence of Community

The tragedy is when there is no community life made up of authentic, tender relationships. When human beings live isolated in collectivities without a soul, how can they ever learn to integrate their sexuality, especially in a society which, through its mass media, continually emphasises sexual needs and at the same time banalises sexual relationships, failing to demonstrate what is sacred in a true relationship and commitment of love?

We need continually to be reminded of the sacred aspect of sexuality. If we vulgarise sexuality and the emotional life, we deny the sacred value of the human heart; we risk destroying it; and in so doing, we destroy the 'house', the 'temple', the body which was made to welcome the gift of God. We cannot destroy God, but we can destroy people who are capable of receiving God.

Some people affirm that the Church and religious leaders have no right to speak of genital sexuality because many of them are celibates. Experience has shown me that many lay men and women as well as priests and ministers often have a great under-standing of the human heart through the thousands of confidences of spiritual direction. Many of them can have more knowledge of the demands and difficulties of love than psychologists. They have received these confidences not only in the light of psychology and human science, but also in the light of the intimate and spiritual consciences of people.

The sacred aspect of the genital sexual life must be announced, but such announcements should be accompanied by a call to create community. Without community, without true rela-tionships, without forgiveness, without celebration, it is not easy to integrate genital sexuality in committed relationships. Without a community life one risks becoming the prey of one's own sexual urges or those of others, the prey of all kinds of seductions, or else one can hide behind thick walls, frightened of relationships.

This is why in our times it is so necessary to work at all costs to create communities, different forms of community such as parish communities, which welcome lonely and marginalised people who have the greatest need to live in a network of friend-ship where they will find their place and be valued.

The Need for Models

In order for people with intellectual disabilities to live their single-ness positively and with serenity, it is valuable for them to know men and women who have truly welcomed celibacy with peace and as a gift from God. If they see single assistants or educators who only begrudge their situation, they will have more difficulty in assuming their own singleness. Married assistants, through their love, can give stability to those with disabilities. The peace and warmth of their family life can be a source of deep healing for their hearts. But they cannot be real models for those who cannot marry.

To be single can be difficult for people with disabilities but it can be equally difficult for some assistants. Many assistants come to l'Arche searching, like so many of the young of our times. They are often fragile in their emotional development; they also sincerely want to be committed to the struggle for a better world. This fragility and a certain idealism often go together. But the experience of living with our core members, in a community inspired by a Christian faith, touches their own hearts. Their inner selves are strengthened and they discover solid motivations for the direction of their lives. Their hearts are awakened in the relationship with someone with a learning disability whose poverty, childlike confidence and cry to be loved are like an invitation, a call, to enter into a relationship involving the gift of their life in fidelity.

Many assistants come to l'Arche attracted by our community life, inspired by the Beatitudes and by the relationship with people with disabilities which lies at the heart of the community. The beginnings are often life-giving. The assistants discover real fraternity; their hearts are touched; many of their own capacities of love and tenderness are revealed which until then had been hidden. As the years go by, however, they become more aware of their own limits and the limits of the community. This is the moment of truth! Often at this time, assistants can start to discover not only their need to grow in greater wisdom, competence and maturity, but also their need for a greater dependence on the Holy Spirit. In the depths of their own hearts they discover the presence of God and a call to live with Jesus in the poor; a profound change can come about by this experience of faith. They discover that the commitment to the poor has to be nourished by prayer, the Word of God and the body of Christ in the Eucharist. Throughout this period of discovery they need to be supported in truth by a priest or minister or another man or woman of God.

A short while ago, a young assistant in one of our l'Arche communities came to see me. She spoke to me of her journey in community. This young woman is competent and deeply present to those in her home. But she herself is fragile at the level of her emotional life. She lives close to anguish, having suffered much in her childhood. She has known intimate relationships with a number of men during her life. She is so afraid of being alone, and afraid of her own emptiness. She has a desperate need to be listened to and to be loved. Her work with and her presence to those who have a disability have nourished her and helped her to structure herself, but not sufficiently to bring her emotional life to maturity. At the same time, she is aware that her pursuit of men lacks authenticity and that she is using her sexuality to attract men to her in order to fill her own emptiness and to escape from loneliness. Her anguish and her call for affection impedes her growth, keeps her from finding her inner strength and from achieving true inner liberty and autonomy. She told me that she felt the need to put an end to these affectionate, but immature relationships in order to grow further. It is evident that her meeting with Jesus and her life of prayer have helped her to be freer *vis-à-vis* her psychological tendencies and her hunger to be loved.

This young woman, product of a broken family, is quite typical of so many other young people and so many of those with disabilities. She needs to be strengthened through prayer, through the challenges and joys of community life, through her personal contact with the poor and serving them. She will have to struggle with her psychological desires in order to grow into a real and more generous love. Then, one day, she will be able to see clearly and respond to God's call to marriage or to celibacy.

The problem of the young is their emotional fragility. Their hearts are rich in the capacity to love. They are intuitive; they see clearly the dangers and the hypocrisies of our world and of so many of the political movements and social organisations, and even church organisations which do not reflect the gospel values. They yearn to live authentic lives. They feel so vulnerable and powerless in front of the forces which shape society and the world. They need examples to encourage and strengthen them. They need those who, by the witness of their lives, invite others to a permanent commitment. Often they do not find such models. Confronted with the gap between their fragility and their ideals, they fall into discouragement and anguish. Some of them come to l'Arche seeking a refuge or even an escape into the spiritual world. Some will need psychological support, in order to find the stability necessary for growth.

All those who find hope in l'Arche have to pass through certain stages, and sometimes through difficult stages, before they can truly put down their roots in the community. The crucial question for many of them is celibacy. Is it possible? Their own emotional needs are so deep!

Some assistants find their fulfilment through marriage and others discover celibacy, not as an indeterminate period of waiting, but rather as a gift of God. This discovery may take long years of maturation before they can live celibacy in response to a deep call from God. Then they can say 'yes' with as much joy and enthusiasm as those who marry. They discover that it is much easier when they have made this decision clearly, relying on the faithfulness and love of God, than when they were still in a state of indecision. This welcome of celibacy as a response to a call of God, and a call of the poor, implies that they have spoken with a man or woman of God who has confirmed them in this choice. It also implies that they have decided to dedicate their capacities for human love to God who is hidden in the hearts of those who are weak and cannot fend for themselves. The decision to say 'yes' does not mean a hardened heart or an escape from relationships into the spiritual or into hyperactivity of service.

On the contrary, it is made so that one may live more fully a committed relationship with people who are weak and vulnerable. When the heart is open to Jesus as a beloved friend, we become more sensitive to human suffering, closer to others, more welcoming and more loving towards them. However, once we have welcomed this gift of celibacy, that does not mean there is no more suffering or questions, for in this area of the emotional life, the heart always remains vulnerable. In l'Arche, our life leads us to lower the walls around our hearts so that we may be open to the tenderness of relationships and live a communion of hearts with our brothers and sisters who have suffered. We do not hide our hearts or protect them. This willingness to be vulnerable brings a great richness to relationships, but it can also create insecurity and a fear of being hurt. We are only able to live this insecurity if the heart is rooted in Jesus and in those who are weak, and if we seek, in the Body of Christ, the Eucharist and prayer, an encounter with the One who loves us and calls us by name to fidelity to those with whom we are bonded. The suffering of a celibate can become, at this point, a sign of his or her love. It is a gift and an offering of the whole self to Jesus and to his friends.

What is specific, however, in l'Arche is that the celibacy of assistants springs frequently from their covenant bonds with the core members. Many of the latter cannot get married; their singleness is imposed upon them. The call of Jesus to celibacy for some assistants is thus linked to this covenant bond with those in distress and in pain. Their celibacy springs from the love that binds them together in the heart of God. It is the communion with people with disabilities that nourishes our heart and sustains us.

My Own Experience of Vulnerability

My personal experience shows me my own need of community and of prayer if I am to live in celibacy. When I am in my community with those whom I love and who love me, I am completely at peace. I experience an inner wholeness. I am able to love with my heart, confident that it will be received without the risk of division or turmoil. In personal encounters, there is often a very great peace, a depth of silence, which is, I believe a sign of the presence of God. In these moments my heart is vulnerable, but at the same time, there is a strength and a unity within me.

On the other hand, when I am travelling alone, far from the community, and if I do not remain in prayer and in contact with my own centre and the presence of Jesus, I can experience a sense of tremendous vulnerability and fragility. I have the feeling of being tossed about by all kinds of winds, attracted by any kind of seduction. Sometimes I have the impression of having neither the strength of will nor the virtue to protect myself. In these moments, I try to entrust myself to God. I pray that he will protect me and keep me from all harm. But I experience a very great poverty.

When I reflect on these moments of poverty, two things become clear. Firstly, I realise that in the intensity of community life I have learned to let my barriers fall, which allows me to be myself. I have learned to live with my vulnerability in order to welcome the other and to show that I truly love him or her.

When I was a naval officer, I had the impression of having more 'virtue' and more 'will', but I was not vulnerable. It was as if I had hidden myself behind barriers and a façade of strength and power, and a fear of relationships. Living in community, we learn not to hide any longer; barriers are not necessary because we have confidence in one another. Thus, when we leave the community, we feel exposed in our vulnerability, especially when our hearts no longer feel protected by an inner peace coming from the presence of God. This confirms me in the knowledge that, even if sometimes I must travel and experience my vulnerability in its nakedness, my life is meant to be lived in community. I need the community in order to live on a certain level of truth and inner liberty. Without it I can become too close to anguish and feel insecure. I feel far from those who are strong, virtuous, and self-willed. I feel more at home with weak and vulnerable people, like myself.

Secondly, I have discovered that the anguish I experience when I am alone, isolated, and vulnerable is favourable ground for the forces of evil. In some way I sense the meaning of the words of St John on the subject of Judas: 'Satan entered into him.' Sometimes the anguish so impoverishes me that I realise that, without God's protection, Satan would provoke me to do the most foolish things. This experience of my poverty and the darkness within me could discourage me; in reality, it does not, but it calls me to live community more fully, and to grow in truth and trust in God.

Celibacy and the Mystery of Love

Community life with its celebrations and its sense of sharing is not enough. We all need unique and personal relationships. I am deeply moved by the sensitivity of heart in some of the men and women with disabilities that I have known, like David who deeply loves Rachael, a young assistant who left to live in a developing country. Time and again, he sends her part of his salary 'for the children with learning disabilities in her centre'. He says: 'Rachael is my friend; it is because of her that I work.' I sense the power and delicacy of the love in his heart as something sacred and divine. This is not a dream, for this love has truly helped him to find a profound balance. It is his secret, and it must be respected.

There is a similar secret in the heart of Richard. He is not a very religious man. He believes, but rarely goes to Mass or to evening prayer. One day, whispering in my ear, he asked me to go with him to the chapel to pray. There he said a prayer of consecration to the Blessed Virgin Mary, putting himself totally in her hands. I was deeply touched by this gesture.

Laurence, too, never goes to Mass except for funerals, weddings and important feast days. This is not because he has anything against the Mass; he is simply not in the habit of going. However, he was very touched by the story of Our Lady of La Salette, the apparition of Mary to two children who saw her weeping. 'She was like a mother beaten by her children and driven from her home,' one of the children said after the apparition. When I welcomed Laurence to l'Arche, he, too, had wept many tears. There was a kind of complicity between him and that woman who had wept on the mountain. It is the secret of his heart.

Many men and women I know in l'Arche have a secret in the depths of their hearts, a secret through which they are linked with someone of the other sex. Whether this person plays the role of father or mother, of big brother or big sister or a beloved for them is not important. What is important is that they love.

I am shocked when I see some people ridiculing the bonds of love which unite a man and a woman with disabilities. Often these are bonds of a secret and sacred tenderness which must be respected. Perhaps they are called to live these bonds only on the level of the heart, in the simplicity of love. It should not be assumed that this relationship must necessarily become physical and sexual as such.

One day in our community in Tegucigalpa (Honduras) I was sitting next to Gloria. She had been truly transformed by her life in l'Arche. I asked her: Gloria, why are you so happy?' After a rather prolonged silence she said 'God'. Later I asked Nadine who was the founder of the community: 'Did you hear Gloria? What do you feel she meant?' Nadine answered: 'That's her secret.' This was not a superficial comment but rather the expression of a deep respect for Gloria.

The heart is so beautiful, so innocent … but it can be betrayed, scorned, broken, seen as unimportant. I remember Laurence, a man about twenty-five years old, who was marked by a very unhappy past. Strictly speaking, one could say that his disability is mild, but since he was put in an institution at a very early age, he had a terribly wounded heart. His mother had abandoned him and her home when he was still a very small child. His father, whom he loved very much and who had brought him up, had to be admitted to a psychiatric hospital. This was the time when Laurence himself was placed in an institution. He was full of anger and violence. Even if he found l'Arche better than the institution, he was not really happy with us. At table he would often explode. One day he met Christine, a young woman with a slight learning disability but very disturbed emotionally. She seduced him. In approaching him with tenderness, she awakened his heart. It was astonishing to see in the space of a few months, the change which took place in him. He became more gentle, more calm; his face became peaceful and relaxed; at table, he would listen to others; his aggression seemed to have melted away.

In obtaining information about Christine who lived in

another centre, the team discovered that she was a dangerous woman in the context of her relationships with men. She would attract a man in order to control him and get him to give her money and gifts, and then would drop him for another. The team did not know what to do. Finally, they decided to let events run their course and they prepared themselves to carry and support Laurence when Christine dropped him. That is what happened, and Laurence fell into depression: he closed in on himself again, even more than before. This experience confirmed his mistrust and fear of women. But, it was amazing to have seen the beauty of his heart. Loved in his being as a man, he had been transformed, though only for a time. Love is the most beautiful reality, but a reality which can also be destructive if it is not an authentic love founded on a commitment.

The sexual life, if it is not lived in a covenant given by God, can obscure the heart, render it opaque. Sexuality can be a sacrament of relationship, but it also can be the death of relationship. The kiss can obstruct the word, that word which is absolutely necessary to deepen the relationship. The sexual instinct is so powerful that it can carry a couple to physical union without going through the stages of friendship and sharing needed in order to know each other. Such a union has no solid foundation or depth on which the future can be built.

The Mystery of Love with Jesus

The more I advance in age, and perhaps in a little wisdom, as I listen to those who have suffered and those who are growing in freedom, the more I am confirmed in my faith in Jesus and in my belief that only God can heal the human heart. I see with more and more clarity that the greatest human suffering is isolation, turning in on oneself, and a lack of love. In discovering their darkness and anguish, some people are engulfed in sadness. Others react and develop a super-ego; their anguish and vulnerability become an energy, driving them to success, domination and power; they become aggressive and always want to be noticed.

Others seek compensations in superficial relationships in violence, alcohol, or drugs; they try to forget and to run away from their darkness. They seek frantically to fill up their inner emptiness.

Who can help us human beings to welcome our own fragility, which is hidden behind the barriers of our fears? Who can help us to assume the flaws of our history and our being, our agonies and weaknesses, even our mortality? We are so very poor: humanly, psychically, morally and spiritually, and we are all bound into that radical poverty: death. We all carry within us a depth of guilt.

Can humanity be saved? Or is it rather condemned to compromise, to untruth, to conflict and to war? Neither science nor technology is able to save humanity. They do not have the means to liberate hearts, opening them to love and sharing. Psychoanalysis is able to free certain blockages, but it cannot change a heart of stone into a heart of love; it is not able to give life, hope and a taste for sharing. War and violence cannot bring peace: they engender hate and vengeance. And salvation cannot come through politics, because a change of structures touches only the exterior; it is our egotistic human hearts which need to be transformed.

I believe that God can change the interior life of our hearts, through the revelation that we are loved, and lovable, that we are of value, and loved by God, just as we are, with all our resistance and our darkness as well as with all our gifts. There is no need to be perfect; we are – each one of us is a beloved child of God, called to become a dwelling place for God. In loving us, God gives us life and the strength to grow ever deeper in love towards a new wholeness. Tagore, the Bengali poet and mystic, writes of how he was called to be the 'dwelling place', the sanctuary of God:

Life of my life, I shall ever try to keep my body pure
knowing that thy living touch is upon all my limbs.
I shall ever try to keep all untruths out from my thoughts,
knowing that thou art that truth which has kindled the
    light of reason in my mind
I shall ever try to drive all evil away from my heart and

keep my love in flower,
knowing that thou hast thy seat in the innermost shrine
   of my heart.
And it shall be my endeavour to reveal thee in my actions,
knowing it is thy power that gives me strength to act.

(Gitanjali 4)

The Father so loved humans in their fragility, their fears and their wounds that he sent his Son, the Word, to reveal his love. He sent Jesus, born of the woman, Mary, to announce to all men and women, whatever their culture, abilities or disabilities, that each one is loved, that no one need be alone or lost. This is the good news: the answer to our anguish and isolation. With him and in him, it is possible to live just as we are, to welcome our disabilities, our deficiencies, our wounds; even to accept our mortality and to have hope and to grow in openness, love and wisdom.

Jesus is the intermediary *par excellence,* who came to reveal to each of us in the secret of our hearts: 'Fear not, I love you; you have value in my eyes; you are able to live; come, advance along the road of life to become, in your turn, an intermediary who will reveal to others that they are forgiven and loved.' Jesus is there, present in the heart of each one of us, but we often are afraid of him, and so we continue to run away or hide behind noise and all sorts of commotion. We refuse to enter into our inner selves to listen to him, the Silent Lover, hidden in the centre of our being. We find it hard to believe that he is hidden in the vulnerability of our hearts, deeper than the anguish and the fear, far deeper than the walls we have built around this vulnerability and the wounds within us.

When we discover that we are loved with an eternal love, with a love beyond all time and space, which goes even beyond death, then everything begins to change, all becomes possible, all can be accepted and loved.

The healing of a person comes, above all, through a personal union with Jesus who has revealed that he is the Friend and the Beloved who touches, awakens and fills the heart.

It is true that the revelation of the love of God almost always comes through a relationship with someone, and in the heart of a community. But the community can never reach and touch a person in a total way; only a person can touch deeply another person. In a community, there is not the covenant of one person with another as in marriage or in the parent–child relationship. The covenant of community, profound as it is, can never guarantee that a certain person will always stay physically close to another. It guarantees only that there will always be someone there, inspired by the same spirit. When the human heart finds Jesus and lives with him in a covenant relationship, it is more inclined to live a covenant relationship in marriage or in community. Someone with disabilities who is sometimes so limited and whose heart is so full of inner pain has a greater need than others to encounter God and hear the Good News of love. There is so little possibility of choosing marriage. Such a person experiences a deep poverty. He or she is unable to fend totally for him or herself, and is in need of others, but above all, in need of Jesus. The Good News permits those who are fragile and wounded in their hearts to discover their deepest identity and vocation, and to discover their place in the community and in the Church.

Society gives the first places to the rich and powerful, to those who are productive and useful. In this system, those with disabilities are always in the last place, if they have a place at all. Frequently they are killed by the inhumanity or ignorance of humans at the moment of their birth if not before, or they are cast aside as they begin to grow up. If they are given even that last place, it is given grudgingly because it is expensive for society.

The Gospel is announced to the poor. The poor are at the heart of the new structure; the first place belongs to them, theirs is the Good News of the presence of Jesus, the Good News which is rejected, most of the time, by the rich and the busy who are satisfied with themselves.

Celibacy as a call from God remains a mystery. It is recognised as a vocation in many religions, even in the religion of ancient Rome; thus it has been shown as a special way of uniting oneself with God and preparing oneself to receive a new and more intimate union with God. Jesus spoke about it very discreetly when, in answering the disciple's question about whether it is expedient to marry if one has to remain with one woman, he said:

> Not everyone can accept what I am saying, but only those to whom it has been given. There are eunuchs born so from birth; there are eunuchs made so by human agency and there are those who have made themselves eunuchs for the sake of the kingdom. Those who can receive this, let them receive it (Matthew 19:11–12).

Celibacy for the sake of the Kingdom, answering the call of Jesus, has always been lived in the Church by those who were chosen by God, and given the grace to be able to welcome it, and to choose it. I believe that Jesus wishes to come in a special way to the aid of those who have no choice in their sinfulness. He wants to touch them in the depths of their hearts, bringing them the peace of a new love. It is true that the Good News is announced to the poor, but it is essential that they have a milieu where they are able to receive and live this Good News. It is important that someone with a learning disability comes to know that celibacy can be welcomed as a gift of God through which the heart can be fulfilled.

This is not to say that all this takes place without suffering. It takes time to heal the heart and for the barriers of fear to come down and to find the balance in relationships. Some people never fully achieve this, engulfed as they are in anguish, depression and even violence. Sometimes they even have to leave the community. For others, the challenge demands much effort, and growth takes many years with moments of progress and moments of failure, during which they need much support and friendship. Their hearts always seem to remain vulnerable. Some, however, seem truly to discover Jesus, the beloved of their hearts. They live at certain moments an authentic experience of the love of God, their hearts burning with that love.

Personally, I am astonished to see, in my own community

where the workshops and so many of the homes are mixed, how much peace there is in the area of sexuality. The way of life, the dynamism of community life, the quality of the assistants and the spiritual life all contribute to this peace. Of course, there are sufferings, disturbances, ambiguities, but in general those with intellectual disabilities seem to enjoy a freedom of heart that few other people in the world attain.

My experience, and the confidences which I have received throughout the years, show me that a spiritual guide can play an important role in this calming of the heart, in the growth in love, in the acceptance of one's disability and in the hope of being able to overcome it realistically. The spiritual guide or accompanier as confidant and as a presence of Jesus in the sacrament of reconciliation becomes a support and a privileged companion. But many people, even spiritual guides and priests, are unaware of the important role which they have concerning the integration of genital sexuality and the growth of love, not only for people with disabilities but for all believers; in addition, they often fail to see their role in calling others to live celibacy as a sign of the Kingdom and as a personal meeting place with Jesus.

The Assistants and the Mystery of Love

Much that has been said about those with learning disabilities, can also be said about the assistants. Their hearts, too, are thirsty for a special love with someone. And, like the young woman of whom we spoke earlier, they have their struggles. They must learn to fix their priorities. They must know what they want and say 'yes' to growth, to the efforts and struggles it implies; they must find help to remain faithful in times of trial or temptation; they must discover the meaning of covenant.

God can unite a man and a woman in a special love which does not to lead to marriage, but strengthens them in celibacy as a gift of God. In these bonds, the woman's heart is awakened and protected by the man just as the man's heart is awakened and protected by the woman.

This special relationship, which is not exclusive, far from distracting them from their vocation, calls them to go even further on the road to wholeness, holiness and communion with those who are weak and rejected. This love reveals itself to be fruitful. Francis de Sales, bishop of Geneva, wrote to Jeanne de Chantal, who later became the foundress of the Visitation Order, that when he thought of her in prayer it was not a distraction from God, on the contrary, it plunged him even deeper into the Holy Trinity. Similarly, Francis of Assisi received life and strength from Clare and Clare from Francis. Thérèse of Lisieux seemed to find life in the relationships she lived with two seminarians with whom she was in correspondence.

I know a deeply prayerful thirty-five-year-old woman who was paralysed in both legs, but her heart and mind have always been very much alive. She confided to me her story, her secret. In one of the many hospitals she spent time in she had met a man who was a gangster, a member of the mafia. He was about to be operated on and was seriously sick. Something deep happened between the two of them. She fell in love with him. After he left the hospital, he would occasionally phone her. She held him in her heart and mind and prayed intensely for him. She knew that there would never be any future to this relationship and yet it inspired her and gave her life. It was for her a gift of God which gave special meaning to her life. It was not just a question of imagination or of the world of fantasy. This relationship opened her up, gave her peace and brought her closer to God. I have met men and women consecrated to God in their celibacy who lived similar, yet different situations and relationships. Their mutual love called them to give themselves more totally to others and to God. They rarely met but their love inspired them, gave them greater strength, nourished and fulfilled them in some way and brought them closer to God. It is clear to me that they were living a communion of hearts that flowed from God and led them into a love which is God.

Today perhaps more than ever before, celibacy is questioned, ridiculed and made difficult to live. I wonder whether it will be more and more frequent for people to have a deep experience of friendship and of love with another that springs from the heart of God in order for them live their celibacy for Jesus and for those who are marginalised. Such love is a free gift of God and, like all gifts, it implies sacrifice and renunciation. We so quickly take the gifts of God for granted and consider them as our right. If God gives this love, he wants us to live it fully in joy and also in abandonment with regard to the future.

One of the difficulties of welcoming and living celibacy in l'Arche is that, strictly speaking, celibacy has no status outside religious life, in which one pronounces vows and makes a solemn profession. Then there is a celebration in which the religious community, family and friends take part. This public announcement is a support for most of the people in l'Arche, however, the declaration of celibacy which has been imposed because of a disability, would have little meaning, unless it was a declaration of a happy, free choice not to marry. This is happening, however, more and more in some communities of l'Arche. The declaration of the person with a disability to choose the community as her family, sometimes with a declaration of a choice not to marry, is often made in the company of assistants who announce the same thing. To date, this has been done by a very small number of persons, but with the existence of special retreats for persons with a disability, it may become more and more common.

In one of our communities in India, a Hindu man with a real but mild disability announced that he had become a Brahmacharya, that is to say, one who renounces the bonds of marriage in order to consecrate all things to God. In general, a Brahmacharya presides over the Puja, the offering of fruits and flowers to God. This decision gave him peace, even if it was his parents who pushed him into it. Then he added: 'Anyway, it is better not to be married, because it is difficult to live with a woman!' Nevertheless, he had found a structure for living his celibacy and for announcing it. It was important because, in India, those who are not married are so often considered inferior.

There is no option like this in Western countries, where there remains a lack of social status for people who are single and are not priests or religious, which makes the acceptance of that state more difficult, both for those with disabilities as well as for assistants. To the extent that community life shared by celibate men and women is recognised as socially acceptable (and this is not always the case), it may help them to live their celibacy in a more positive way. The welcome of celibacy is very personal, touching the very fragility of one's being at different moments and ages in one's life. But we must ensure the structures, the friendship, the mutual aid, the dynamism, the love in community life and the spirituality which will allow people to live their celibacy peacefully and with joy.

In the hearts of each one of us, whether we are married or single or celibate, there are moments of anguish, disturbance, frustration, isolation, sometimes even disequilibrium in the genital sexual life. There are times of fear, of escape, times when we cry out in anguish and which we are called to accept as part of our journey in life. We are not yet in paradise. We hope to attain for ourselves and for each other, a maximum of peace, of happiness, of love and of balance. One day we will live that transition when we are broken and stripped of everything: death. Death awaits us. Death can become our friend. Francis of Assisi spoke of 'sister death'. Happiness, if it is in personal and community fulfilment, in the celebration of unity and our love for one another, is also in the waiting, beyond the transition of death, for that gift to come: the wedding feast of Heaven, meeting Jesus face to face and heart to heart and being in total communion with his friends and lovers.

Chapter Seven

UNITY IN MARRIAGE

During our community's recent 'Open House' I had the joy of meeting three couples of which four of the people with disabilities had been former members of l'Arche. We talked and laughed together and remembered the 'good old days'. In my heart, I rejoiced in the authentic harmony and peace which reigned in these couples. I knew each one's story, the story before and the story after the marriage, stories marked by suffering, moments of anguish as well as moments of great joy. I remembered ten years earlier, I had gently teased Jean-Paul, one of the men: 'If you don't get your teeth straightened, you'll never get married.' At that time, Jean-Paul was sure that marriage was not for him, so he told me to 'buzz off'! Some years later, he had straightened his teeth ... and then ...

The Birth of an Authentic Relationship

Whether they live together in community or not, there comes a time when a man and a woman with disabilities can be attracted to each other, even though there might not be many verbal exchanges. Perhaps the sufferings of the past and the rejections they have both known create a greater solidarity between them. Often they understand each other with very few words. Little by little, they sense that perhaps they will be able to live together in mutual support and love for each other. They take the step as a couple. Then the question comes up for us: how to help them to walk together, to discern the stages and to deepen their relationship in truth.

It is an extraordinary thing for a man with a disability to discover that he is loved, not only by an assistant, an elder brother or sister, but also by a young woman of his age who is perhaps in the same centre or same community. Something new takes place in his being: he discovers a new dimension of wholeness. Faced with such a development, the educator is called to help both persons to become aware of the beauty of these new bonds of love and, also, the responsibilities which they imply. These bonds must not be taken lightly by the two people or by their parents or educators.

Who Decides What?

In l'Arche, as at any other centre, we (like parents) are confronted by the fact that people with learning disabilities are not usually able to cope by themselves with life on a practical level. Even if there is enough money, they need help filling out forms, reading contracts and so on. They will need to be accompanied by others so that they may have the fullest human life possible. This means that their emotional life is observed, looked at, analysed, sometimes controlled. This is the tragedy. They need permission and direction. In every way this can distort things. If people with disabilities were able to do what they wanted, things would be simpler and more authentic. This was the case with Paul and Marie of whom we will speak later. They had both been classified as having learning disabilities but, in fact they did not. They were perfectly capable of managing by themselves, with a little support. In fact, most of the time, people with learning disabilities look around to know what their elders or their educators think. They are often dependent on their attention and their support. They do not always have the interior strength to say: 'I am going to do it by myself.' The people around a couple with a disability may either encourage and support their relationship or else discourage (or sometimes forbid) them from moving towards marriage.

Sometimes it is also the elders or educators who encourage people with learning disabilities to live as a couple and to have sexual relations because they say it is good for them, that 'this couple can be happy and fully human only if they love and fully profit from the exercise of their sexuality.' At the same time, however, they may say: 'Above all, no children.' They may even administer contraceptives or, if a child is conceived, demand an abortion. Thus it was that Emmanuelle (of whom we will speak in chapter 8), had to battle with her educators to keep her child.

So many people with learning disabilities are not free. Their disability makes them so dependent on others. It is the responsibility of the team of educators or assistants to lead them into living with the greatest independence possible. Thus it is that at l'Arche, as elsewhere, we take decisions for others which affect their lives. It is true that we encourage some couples to move towards marriage and discourage others. Of the three couples I mentioned earlier, those who were former members of l'Arche had left their home in l'Arche to live more independently. It was from this more independent living that they moved towards marriage.

The Beauty and the Seriousness of Sexual Relationships

It is true that in l'Arche we do not want to belittle sexual relationships. We do not believe that they are just a therapeutic means, or a way for someone to express himself and to liberate a physical need. We believe in the beauty, in the gravity and, I would say the mystery of sexuality as an expression of a profound communion between two persons and the gift of their being to each other, in a reciprocal and permanent commitment. We believe that when this is not the case, and when the sexual act is completely separated from the relationship of communion between two people, it is no longer a source of unity for them. When the sexual act is separated from the heart and from relationship, the other person becomes an object. There is no longer anything personal in the act. There is no giving; only taking. The sexual act in this context loses the beauty of its potential to deepen the unity and affection of the couple.

To affirm such a belief is an enormous challenge in these times when sexuality is so vulgarised by the mass media and when others propose that those with disabilities should be given every help and material means to exercise their right to sexuality and to pleasure. My fear today is that, instead of helping those with disabilities to discover the love of a couple, with all its intimacy and the bond it implies, they are led towards the mirage of easy sexuality without responsibility, without a permanent bond between two people, without true fecundity. This form of sexuality finally leads them to disappointment and a new isolation, because it does not respond to their deepest needs, to their thirst for a covenant relationship. The attraction of man for woman, and of woman for man, is profound. There is a thirst for tenderness which nourishes itself through sexuality and which leads to it. But, for that sexuality to be truly human, springing up from relationship and strengthening it, people must have a clear awareness of their identity, knowing who they are and what they wish to make of their lives. It is essential that there be a desire to share one's life in a permanent way with another. Those who exercise their sexuality without having an emotional maturity, without knowing what is actually sought in a sexual relationship, can aggravate their state of confusion. Far from developing a sense of identity, it can be diminished.

We are touching here the heart of the problem which separates the position of l'Arche from other options. We esteem genital sexuality as a beautiful and powerful reality which calls forth the person in the depths of his or her being. It is a means of exceptional fruitfulness, a unique means of expression: it is not something superficial. It is not another activity in the weekly program such as meals or sports or yoga.

The unique friend – the husband or the wife – is not simply a partner as in a sport. He or she is the beloved, the chosen one of the heart, to whom one entrusts that which is most intimate in one's body and in one's heart. The exercise of sexuality leads to a new relationship. The values of gift and communion implied in the gestures of love carry with them something absolute. This reciprocal gift of one to the other liberates them from the power of self-centredness and opens them both more deeply to others, to justice, to peace-making, to the universe and to God. In this way, they become for each other, not an idol of worship, but an icon, a sign of the presence of God.

In the Christian vision, this mutual gift of the man and the woman, this new bond through the body and genital sexuality, is so profound that it is acknowledged as the image of that which unites Christ with his Church: 'Husbands should love their wives just as Christ loved the Church and sacrificed himself for her ... For this reason, a man must leave his father and mother, and be joined to his wife, and the two will become one body. This mystery has many implications; but I am saying it applies to Christ and the Church' (Ephesians 5:25, 31–32). The most authentic Christian version does not deny, condemn, or devalue genital sexuality; on the contrary, it sees it as a reality so beautiful and so profound that it can be lived fully and most humanly only if the two persons recognise the bonds which unite them forever; these are a covenant, founded on the covenant of each one with God.

In Daily Life

Genital sexuality is a sign of love and friendship, of gift and communion. Because of this it involves all of life. Sexual relationships are like the summit, a celebration of unity because it does not happen at the very beginning of the relationship. It is not what happens the moment that two people meet. There is a journey of ever deepening familiarity and affection which leads more and more to the desire of giving oneself, of unity with the other. But this summit means there must be a base, a daily life together, a life in common. This requires a milieu which is 'home'.

Through the exercise of genital sexuality, people give themselves to one another in their hearts and in their bodies. The body is the place of physical intimacy, which signifies the intimacy of hearts. The body given by one becomes precious to the other, it is the body of the beloved. In this relationship, which implies and calls forth a covenant, one becomes, in some way, responsible for the body of the other. We become responsible for that which we tame, says the fox in Saint Exupéry's *The Little Prince*. We love the other in his or her body and spirit not only when he or she is healthy, but also when he or she is weak and tired. The love which is contained in the body not only rejoices in the encounter: it also desires to carry the other, to support and help him or her in times of trial; it is service and kindness in daily life. As John Paul II so strongly expresses it:

> ... sexuality by means of which man and woman give themselves to one another through the acts which are proper and exclusive to spouses, is by no means something purely biological, but concerns the innermost being of the human person as such. It is realised in a truly human way only if it is an integral part of the love by which a man and woman commit themselves totally to one another until death. The total physical self giving would be a lie if it were not the sign and fruit of a total personal self giving in which the whole person, including the temporal dimension, is present. If the person were to withhold something, or reserve the possibility of deciding otherwise in the future, by this very fact he or she would not be giving totally.[1]

Sexuality lived as covenant serves life: through it the family is built in the service of the little one, the child. It is here that sexuality finds its fullest meaning, that it makes a man and a woman co-creators with God to give life to another human person. It is through this that the couple open themselves to a reality which is beyond them: when a man and a woman discover themselves capable of giving life, capable of putting themselves profoundly in the service of a fragile little being, capable of becoming parents. This opening frees them from the possibility of becoming a couple closed in on itself.

The sexual relationship, when cut off from daily life, is torn up from its roots and does not bear fruit. It is but a moment of excitement, of contact, of pleasure cut off from reality. It does not involve responsibility with regard to the other. The risk is that it is lived, more or less, like a game; it is not a sign of commitment. It is not the gesture of tenderness and trust between two people linked in a profound way. Thus, in the unconscious, fear persists. The exercise of sexuality risks becoming a tactic of seduction in order to keep the other, or a tactic of seduction that affirms my power to seduce; a sign of sexual conquest, prowess – where the other is merely an object. If I lose my beauty or dynamism, will you leave me? The exercise of genital sexuality without a recognised and expressed commitment remains fragile, subject to the moods, the fears and the passions of one or the other, and to constant doubt: 'You love me because I please you today, but do you truly love me for myself?'

For those with learning disabilities in a group home or residence, the risk of isolation when one is abandoned by one's partner does not take the same form as it does for those who, having been abandoned, have to live alone. Obviously they can often be terribly disappointed and hurt as a result of the failure of the relationship.

To facilitate the exercise of genital sexuality in a residence without taking any responsibility for the other person or for running a home and bringing up children, can debase sexuality, reducing it to the most superficial and exterior level. To do this with persons who have a disability is to devalue their humanity.

Difficulties in Living Covenant Relationships in Marriage

To live an authentic covenant in marriage is not without great difficulties. It is important not to ignore them. Many, in the euphoria of honeymoon and marriage, forget the loss and grieving that are also an aspect of any covenant. In attaching oneself to one man or one woman, one, in effect, renounces all other men and women. In rooting oneself in one land, one renounces all other lands. In giving oneself to one person, one loses the freedom to give oneself to others.

This grief, this loss of liberty, is necessary in order to welcome a new liberty, the liberty of giving oneself totally and without restraint to another which is discovered in a covenant relationship. It is the liberty of paternity and maternity, the liberty of knowing oneself to be loved and capable of love.

The beginnings of a deep and intimate relationship between a man and a woman are often full of joy; everything is euphoric. Many of the barriers built around their hearts, which until now held them in a certain reserve and isolation, fall down. They are liberated from their fears and their anguish, from all that kept them from expressing themselves. However, after a certain time, clouds can appear in the relationship. In the beginning, the light of one called forth the light of the other. Then the light of one touches the darkness of the other, and finally the darkness of one touches the darkness of the other. They get on each others' nerves and become blocked in their relationship one to the other. Because of the deepening intimacy, and the accompanying vulnerability, love risks being transformed into hate.

The transition from the euphoria of encounter to blockages and inability to communicate with each other is painful. Here is a classic example of what happens. In the early days of marriage, the man leaves his work quickly in order to be with his wife. He speaks freely; he is enthusiastic, attentive, sensitive. Then, little by little, he begins to be more taken up by his work, or some social, political or religious activity. He comes home later and later. He is tired, less enthusiastic. He can then lose himself in television. Perhaps he begins to drink. The wife gives herself more and more to the children; she also works, and, little by little, a wall can grow up between them.

This evolution of the relationship between a husband and wife is well known. These days so many couples are separating and seeking a divorce. The man and the woman find themselves alone, frustrated, angry, depressed, and unable to live in an atmosphere of conflict and aggression. Their hearts are so vulnerable. New relationships are regarded with suspicion or distrust. The wound continues in fears and doubts: 'Will I be able to remain faithful? Will the other remain faithful? Was it my fault or the other's?

Where did I go wrong?' Finally they part.

The man and the woman did not realise that the point of the blockage could instead have been the point of growth. When that which is negative in one touches that which is negative in the other, they may be able to move to a new level in their relationship and their life together with their children, providing they find help to get through the tunnel, or find new inner resources. They need to discover how to communicate in a new way and how to accept the other as he or she changes and evolves with age and in new situations.

The union of the man and the woman, and the life with their children, are there for the growth and healing of each other. They are there to grow together in love and service, towards a true maturity, to be better able to open themselves to others, to the world and to God. They are there to be transformed. This implies that certain barriers and egotistical and egocentric tendencies, built in childhood and reinforced in adolescence, must begin to disappear. This hurts. That is why there is confusion and suffering when one or the other, or both, begin to touch their anguish and begin to experience their limits and the hurts of the other person. It is important that the couple not flee from the difficulties and the anguish, because growth, deepening, and healing would be impeded.

Marriage

But is a covenant relationship between a man and a woman possible? Is love anything more than an euphoric moment which always ends in blockages and hate? Isn't this the experience of so many couples?

I believe that a permanent relationship is possible and strengthened when the heart of each has been touched by God and healing has begun. This encounter with God permits a couple to face better the demands of the relationship. In the past, and even today in some countries, the traditional extended family gave support and stability to the union between man and woman.

Where everyone lives together or very near each other – cousins, brothers and sisters, grandparents, uncles and aunts there can be the very real advantage of advice and counselling, sometimes un-solicited, which is a part of life. The older women can share with the new bride their own experiences and difficulties – and the same among the men. The man and the woman discover that their problems are neither new nor unique. There is support and encouragement, hope that there is indeed light at the end of the tunnel.

One difficulty today is that the isolated couple does not understand that certain painful moments in the relationship are part of a passage that all couples must live. It is not the time to abandon all hope. In the nuclear family, the husband and wife, together with their children, often find themselves very isolated. If their relationship is not one of frequent communication and sharing, it can deteriorate quickly. For a relationship to remain alive, energy, creativity and time are needed. So many couples live in situations where they do not have the support and encourage-ment that they need. As a result they no longer have the energy to deepen their relationship or communicate, and so they drift apart.

The relationship between them is so precious, not only for the two of them but also for the children, for society, for God, that the Father himself has promised always to come and help them as they journey towards a deeper unity. This union between man and woman is sacred. It is in the image of God, the Father, Son and Spirit which is the source of all human unions.

Marriage as a Sacrament

This is why the union of man and woman is called to be a sacra-ment, announced before the community of believers and con-firmed by the Church. It is a sacred sign, instituted by Jesus. It is a place of encounter with God. God is present in this union and always comes to the aid of the spouses. God helps them to profit from all the difficult elements in marriage. Instead of hiding from each other and escaping into work or other activities, instead of becoming aggressive or depressive, they can live a deeper union through the acceptance of daily life with one another. They can live not only the deep joys of this union, but also forgiveness.

Forgiveness is the great gift of Jesus to humanity. Jesus came to pardon us and to show us how to forgive. Forgiveness is the love offered to another who is wounded, vulnerable, fearful and who has broken the unity. Forgiveness implies the understanding that all the blockages, all the aggressive acts come, in great measure, from inner sufferings, anguish, and fears. Forgiveness is the welcome of the other just as he or she is with all the flaws, all the past, all the weaknesses, and all the sin. Forgiveness signifies and acknowledges the covenant with another. Forgiveness is also the recognition and acceptance of one's own lack of love and tenderness and of a real acceptance of the other.

It is this forgiveness coming from the heart of God which heals people in the depths of their being. It is this which progressively transforms the wounded image of self into the positive image of a child of God. It is this which transforms culpability into responsibility and into confidence in oneself, in others, and in God. When one has experienced this forgiveness, he or she is able in turn to forgive.

The sacrament of marriage transforms the foundations of the union between man and woman. It is not only a question of love one for the other, of the promise to give oneself to another for life, but a call and a confirmation of God. The foundations of this union are in the desire of the Father that man and woman, despite their wounds and their psychological and human poverty, should share in his trinitarian life and in his merciful love. The life of the couple, then, is founded on this forgiveness which alone can heal the wounds inflicted on their unity. The road to unity must pass through daily forgiveness. And celebration, which is a sign that forgiveness is total, culminates in the tenderness and union of love. This union of love in spirit and body gradually drives out all aggression and the blockages which might remain, and makes of the two one flesh, one heart, one soul, one spirit ... The union becomes eucharistic, an act of thanksgiving for having refound unity.

This is why the genital organs are sacred. They are reserved for a divine work: to be at the same time a sign of trinitarian life and a source of life. These organs are meant for a life of love in a covenant which has been blessed and confirmed by God. Their usage outside of this covenant relationship can trap the man and the woman each in his or her own isolation. The sexual act, instead of being a source and sign of hope, can become a cause of suffering and despair. It can awaken that which is most intimate, most sacred, most vulnerable in the human heart without being able to fulfil it, or to respond to the deep need to be loved with a total love. When it is enveloped in the presence of Jesus, the love of husband and wife can deepen and bring them profound peace. Their hearts are thirsting, not for a passing love, not for a subjective pleasure, but for a total and eternal love which will bring them out of their isolation into unity.

The tragedy of marriage and the union of bodies in love is that so many enter into it believing that it is going to be paradise and that their deepest needs will be fulfilled. Others, who have had bad experiences, may enter into marriage with cynicism and despair. Truth lies between these two attitudes, between naivety and despair. The human heart thirsts for a paradise and an eternal wedding feast which is not illusory, but one can only enter into happiness in stages. So many of the young who lack maturity believe that perhaps marriage will be this paradise. But then they discover that it is a school of life and of love; it is a place of transformation. Through the joys and the ecstasies, but also through the pain, the blockages, and times of forgiveness, they progressively learn how to love and be faithful. They learn that love is a gift, a beautiful gift, but also that each one has to work at loving. Each one has to see where they have to grow and change. At first, the gift of their tenderness and their bodies is very immature. But because they want their union to be a sign of the presence of God and a sacrament, they grow together in love and truth through this 'work'. Together they become a sign of the Kingdom.

United Christian families are a sign that love, unity and peace are possible. These families are, each in their own way, the first cell of all unity, of all forgiveness, of all community, of all fecundity. They are thus signs of hope.

Marriage for People with Learning Disabilities

It is evident that some people with a disability, especially if it is slight, are able to enter into the joys and pains of a conjugal life and of a family life. Many people who have been labelled 'disabled' could have functioned quite well in society if they had received adequate support. Being categorised as 'disabled' can wound a person and destroy self-confidence. This negative image, of being one who is considered 'different', 'abnormal', is reinforced by parents, by others around them and, finally, by a placement in a specialised centre.

A study carried out by Jacques Servais on the support needed by those with disabilities who marry, provides many examples and a bibliography.[2] It confirms perfectly the experience of the communities of l'Arche, that marriage is possible, but only for a minority of those with learning disabilities.

The right to marry, an inalienable right of everyone, can only be exercised lawfully and lived fully, if its duties express the will to respect and support the partner of the covenant. Moreover, as with all vocations, marriage presupposes attractions and aptitudes. In contemporary society, the accent is generally put on the attraction for marriage rather than on the aptitude. Here, as elsewhere, educators must try to motivate the partners with disabilities to take responsibility for their future. To do this, they must begin by creating a relationship of trust which engenders security, then they can bring constructive criticism and help to the two concerned.[3]

Those who accompany the couple are most often needed to help clarify what is hidden in the desire which has been expressed for marriage, to explain fully the real responsibilities it entails and to ensure that the capacity to face them is developed. Because, as we all know, marriage is never easy. It is a place of growth for the two spouses.

The person who accompanies will have the task of stimulating social, friendly and familial relationships in order to keep the couple from closing in on themselves. The roles of such a person are manifold: to serve as a reference, confidant or counsellor if requested by the couple: perhaps above all to renew confidence in times of difficulty.

In spite of all the problems, statistics and research reveal that there are no more separations or divorces among marriages of those with developmental disabilities than among those regarded as 'normal'.[4] But behind the figures there are very different, and sometimes suffering, realities.

I remember the situation of Paul and Marie. Marie was a woman of about forty who is paralysed down one side and had lived in one of our communities for four years. She was difficult, finding it hard to live in a group if she was not continually the centre of attention, and she knew well how to get it.

Before coming to the community, she had lived at home: a traditional family in which, because of her disability, she had always been hidden. There was no question of her going out to a dance or to visit friends as her younger brothers and sister did. And because of this Marie was angry and bitter. She was never satisfied. Her disability limited her capacity for work, but she dreamed of an independent life. She insisted that the team find her an apartment in the city, although there was no certainty that she was ready for such autonomy. Very quickly, Marie met a man who also had a disability and who had lived in one of our homes but was now living in an apartment and holding a job in competitive employment. They quickly moved in together without telling anyone.

We didn't know what to do. Marie had already had several relationships with men when she lived in the community home. In general, these men were much younger and more limited than she was; her love for them was terribly possessive and quite harmful for the men concerned.

We did not know if Marie was capable of fidelity. Did she love

Paul for himself, or was she simply seeking the status of a 'married woman'? In addition, they both had problems with alcohol. It was difficult to know how to guide them when both, in a very understandable adolescent crisis, affirmed their autonomy by rejecting everyone who came to them from the community. It was then that a couple, friends of the community, befriended them and were able to give them support. Paul and Marie decided to marry. The attitude of Marie's family completely changed once she 'became like everyone else'; she found her place, an equality with her brothers and sister. The first years of the marriage were difficult. Marie finding herself alone all day in the apartment, began to drink more and more. She finally agreed to take part in a detoxification programme, and, for the last two years, their marriage has been much more peaceful.

On reading a report about people placed in a hospital because of their intellectual disability (Pacific State Hospital, California),[5] and then discharged, I was happy to see how many had married more or less successfully. Of the forty-eight people studied, all with fairly mild disabilities, thirty-four had married. Only four of this group had separated from their partner or been divorced. The story of each one is different, but there are certain constants. Those who had been very disturbed at a sexual level before their entry into the hospital, had found inner stability and peace in a committed relationship; and each manifested a certain pride in having a home of their own, a husband or wife. Nearly all the women had been sterilised before they were discharged from the hospital, and they suffered from this. There is no doubt that their desire to escape the label of 'disabled', and to be like everyone else, was the strength which helped them to live their marriage. The anguish of loneliness immediately after they had left the hospital had also been a force which had prompted them to seek and to find a possible partner. And, once married, they were so determined not to fall again into this anguish that they often made considerable sacrifices and adjustments for the sake of their marriage. Maybe it is easier for someone with a learning disability to accept such adjustments than for others more capable, more autonomous, more jealous of their independence and their rights – and less willing to be at the service of the other.

The Child

Obviously, the most delicate question is that of procreation. Can a couple, both of whom have learning disabilities, have children?

This question is complex. We quickly forget that some women with an intellectual disability would like more than anything to be mothers. The suffering of sterility is intolerable for them. If they are encouraged to have sexual relationships and are at the same time prevented from conceiving a child, a profound maternal desire is not being met. This will provoke frustration and anguish. Their deepest desire is not being met.

However, it must be acknowledged that it is not good for some people with an intellectual disability to have a child. Clearly we must not encourage the conception and birth of a child if there is a risk of the child having a severe disability, or not being welcomed, loved and cared for properly. But the problem is not simply a question of heredity. More delicate is the fact that the person may not be able to bring up her child even if it is normal. A mother who has a learning disability is able, of course, to nurse her child and to enjoy looking at him or her but, when the child becomes irritable, difficult, anguished, there is a risk that some mothers may become terribly insecure and anguished themself. At that moment, she may abandon or abuse her child. For a mother to bring up her child she must have a security, a liberty, and an interior peace which is not always the case with some women with learning disabilities. It is irresponsible to let them have children if they are manifestly not able to bring them up adequately.

There again, we can be mistaken. Emmanuelle became pregnant by Christopher, a man with hemiplegia who had lived in one of our homes and who lacked all confidence in himself. Both he and Emmanuelle worked in the same workshop. The staff there urged Emmanuelle to have an abortion. She refused. She absolutely wanted her baby. Christopher was very frightened; he was so lacking in confidence that he didn't believe he could be a husband, let alone a father. But, little by little, he became more peaceful and the two of them decided to marry. Christopher accepted the idea of being a father. Some time before all this, Christopher had left his home in l'Arche, refusing all contact with the assistants. He wanted to go it alone. But, faced with Emmanuelle's pregnancy, the questions of his marriage, and the idea of being a father, he sought out the assistants for counsel and support. Christopher and Emmanuelle are now happy parents. A couple, friends of the community, visit them on a regular basis. A deep friendship has been established between the two couples. They help each other. Their little child seems happy. He is growing up well, and Christopher and Emmanuelle seem to be good parents. It is beautiful to see them.

Jacqueline was in one of our city homes. She became pregnant by a man whom we had welcomed on a trial basis in another home and whom we did not know well. We found a foster home for Jacqueline. Through becoming a mother she made much progress; she became more independent and found work in a factory near her home, something she had not been capable of doing before the birth of her child. She lived with her child; but the couple who had welcomed her acted as parents. This situation, though by no means perfect, was not too bad. It was a human situation. The little one grew and soon surpassed his mother on the intellectual level. This threatened her, and she began to regret having him. Was this the reason she became pregnant a second time, probably by someone at the factory? In speaking with her during this second pregnancy, it seemed evident that she did not wish to bring up her second child. He was born, a beautiful baby, and adopted very young. Then the woman who had welcomed Jacqueline died, and the elderly husband was no longer able to keep her and her first child whom she could no longer tolerate. We found a centre, not far away, which welcomed her first child who is helped by his godfather, a former assistant of l'Arche who was with us during Jacqueline's first pregnancy. We also had to find another foster family for Jacqueline. The situation remains delicate.

Is not this the fragility inherent in the human condition? Jacqueline is surrounded with competent care; it is necessary to continue to walk closely with her.

Michelle sought her independence from the community. She is an intelligent young woman but very wounded in her heart and emotions, and abandoned by her family. When we welcomed her twelve years ago, she was close to psychosis. She has made much progress at a human and social level and in her work. For some time, she has lived alone, working in a factory. She was very happy to be finally on her own, free, 'not having assistants on her back'! But she was seduced by an older man who took advantage of her. She had been attracted to this man who needed her. They did not live together, but they saw each other regularly. She conceived a child and had an abortion. Speaking of this one day with a former assistant, she told her story with a little defiance and pride, insinuating that she was much freer than the assistant. When the assistant asked her whether she had not suffered, Michelle burst into tears, admitting that she had been forced to have the abortion.

I know of three other situations in l'Arche communities, where women have had children. They did not have an abortion. First, because it is serious to kill a child in the mother's womb; and, secondly, because the women themselves did not want an abortion. It is often the educators and parents who do not want a woman for whom they are responsible to have a child. They can manipulate her so that she accepts the abortion. In these three cases the women gave birth to beautiful children. They were able to touch them, to look at them, to admire them, and even to give them a name. In all three situations, the mothers agreed that their little one be adopted.

It is wrong to encourage a young pregnant woman to have an abortion. This causes her to believe that the fruit of her womb is rotten. If her fruit is rotten, then she herself must be rotten. This reinforces the broken image she has of herself and forces her to live with serious guilt. To force her to abort is to cut off the movement of life within her.

It is obvious that all of this is not simple. We are touching an area where there is much human suffering and fragility. I still have many questions on this difficult subject regarding the possibility of those with an intellectual disability to have children. Each situation depends so much on the story and the character of each person, and the on-going support that will be available that it seems to me well nigh impossible to lay down rigid rules.

How can we help a couple who cannot have children or, if they could, are not able to raise a child adequately, to avoid closing in on themselves as so often happens? Will they find, instead of welcome and service of the child which is the natural fruit of a couple, the necessary resources to make their life in common a life open to others and to God? What is the source of strength and hope which will allow them to come to terms with their differences, overcome the conflicts and surpass the difficulties and blockages which are found in daily life? I think that a common vision, which places their life as a couple in a perspective of service, close to a community which will support and motivate them, will give them the best chance to achieve and maintain balance and maturity.

In this area there are many unanswered questions. I think in particular of Didier and Marianne who both have emotional difficulties and intellectual deficiencies. I wouldn't dare to say that they were capable of raising a child. Yet their marriage has brought them both a real well-being and a new stability. They love each other and support each other. Even if there are difficulties, these do not prevent their marriage from being a beautiful reality.

Who Can Get Married?

Finally then, who can be encouraged towards marriage? First, one point must be clear: it must be the couple themselves who decide to marry, never the decision of someone else. In l'Arche we do not speak of marriage to those who, in the abstract, wish to marry. We speak of it to a couple who have already made their own way towards it. Certainly, someone is able to envisage marriage only if he or she is moving toward a real emotional maturity, passing from the stage of attracting everyone to oneself to the stage of opening oneself to another or others, toward a real responsibility for them. This emotional maturity implies that, gradually, the person is becoming capable of a permanent relationship with another person, capable also of helping the other and carrying someone who is in some way weaker.

Of course, there is no such thing as a perfectly self-giving and altruistic love; we always seek in another something for ourselves. Closed in on ourselves, we have a hard time listening and understanding others, and we are even in danger of oppressing and destroying them. But there can be a gradual liberation from egotistical tendencies. Little by little we can be opened as we discover the other as a living person, who has needs and who suffers, a person whom we can help to grow in inner equilibrium and to discover the truth of his or her being, a person we can love and be loved by.

Personally, I have great confidence in those couples who, announcing their desire to marry, take the time to deepen the meaning of their marriage without hastily moving into sexual relations, and who are willing to have someone accompany and counsel them.

Thus, the time of their engagement becomes a time of a deepening discovery of the other, through the heart and through dialogue in which they are able to share their ideas of life, their tastes, their desires, their values. They have time to look at some questions in their life as a couple before they reach a crisis or become an emergency. They are able to reflect together on the changes which will take place in their lives and on the best way to experience these together; this takes place through a course of preparation adapted to their needs and guided by a supportive friend. During this time they can also receive a more complete sexual education which would permit them to know and respect the other more, and to discover the mysterious and sacred dimension of genital sexuality.

A human being, often so poor and fragile, is so rich in unexpected possibilities for growth.

Chapter Eight

FECUNDITY AND THE WELCOME OF DEATH

The Cry for Fecundity

It is clear that the body of man, like that of woman is made as it is in order to maintain humanity on earth. Their differences and their mutual attraction are necessary for life and in order to give life. The link between genital sexuality and procreation is so profound, that for a long time moralists and theologians saw fecundity as the only goal of sexual union, putting aside this union as the expression of intimate love, or assigning it to a secondary place. In our times, however, the connection between sexual relationships and intimacy has been so accentuated that people can put aside the link between genital sexuality and the deeply rooted physical need to continue the existence of human life on earth and to leave behind us another like ourselves. In our rich society, there is a real link between the refusal or fear of death and the refusal and fear of fecundity, of fruitfulness. The desire for procreation, the yearning to have a child, is contained in genital sexuality. Genital sexuality is a response of God to our fear of isolation: 'It is not good that man should be alone.' It is also God's response to our fear of another isolation, that of death: 'Be fruitful and multiply' (Genesis 1:28).

Even when one refuses to have a child, the cry and the desire of nature is so strong and powerful, that despite all precautions, despite all natural or artificial means of contraception, there are still an immense number of unwanted children who are conceived and, alas, aborted.

Biological life is made up of three functions: nourishment, growth, and procreation. Nourishment permits growth by the multiplication of the cells. All growth is directed towards procreation in order that the species continues to exist. All living beings have the means of reproduction and an insatiable need to give life. This need is so powerful that, from generation to generation, vegetation, animals, and human beings reproduce and perpetuate life on earth. Those of ancient cultures saw in this need something divine. Living beings, said Plato and Aristotle, are not immortal in themselves; the individual is mortal, but they participate in immortality through the species, by their capacity to reproduce another like themselves. The desire for immortality is hidden in the cry or the desire for reproduction, for procreation.

The mystery of fecundity implies the desire of the seed to fall into the womb of the earth and the desire of the earth to welcome the seed and to nourish it and call forth new life. This physical and metaphysical desire for reproduction, for procreation, for new birth is a sign of God hidden in living matter. It is the secret of God written into this biological reality. In the attraction of man for woman, and of woman for man, in their loving attention, there is something divine, a thirst for immortality, a desire for fecundity.

There is something extraordinarily beautiful in the conception of a child, but also something so very little and humble. From the moment of fertilisation, the mother in some sense has nothing more to do except to let the process of life continue within her. She cannot even choose the sex of her child.

In human fecundity, biological fecundity is fulfilled through the fecundity of love and caring. It is necessary that the parents welcome with love and tenderness the little one whom they have conceived so that the child can grow and find his or her place in the universe. Human fecundity does not end at birth as is the case with many animals. Parents continue through long years to carry their child, giving life and nourishment and helping him or her to grow in so many ways. It is the parents' love and care which gives the infant security to overcome fear and anguish; it is their love which allows the child, in spite of so much fragility and vulnerability, to find his or her place in the family, and thus in society and in the world.

When we see to what extent children become mentally and psychically blocked, either because of rejection or because of overprotection, we can easily understand how real love is the source of life. One who is loved is able to grow without fear, is able to be oneself and acquire language to communicate, and above all, to develop the capacity to love others.

Sterility is a terrible tragedy for a human being. In psychiatric hospitals and in institutions for chronically sick people, we can sometimes see women who have deliberately made themselves ugly; they dress badly, their hair is a mess, they smell awful: they are so sure that no one could love them, and that they are sterile and incapable of giving life! In ancient civilisations, sterility was sometimes considered a punishment from God. But if biological sterility is painful, spiritual sterility is even more terrible.

Fecundity should not be confused with productivity. We produce, using reason and techniques, an object which does not live. It is a material object to be possessed, used or sold, but it is never an end in itself. Productivity gives power to those who control production.

To be fruitful, to bear fruit, is to give life to another human being. It is a relationship, in love, of one living being with another. We do not possess the little boy to whom we have given life. On the contrary, we give him space to live and the freedom to be himself. It is marvellous to be fruitful; but, there are also responsibilities and risks involved. We cannot do as we like with our child. The situation becomes tragic when parents want to programme and control the whole life of their child. This can provoke deep disturbance. Fecundity implies entering into the whole chain of life which links human beings together throughout history. The child must inevitably overtake his parents in some way and in turn be overtaken by his own children. Life is a continual discovery, uncovering in wonder and unending newness the secrets of God.

The history of humanity is holy because in it the mystery of God is revealed through love and through the struggle against the forces of evil, darkness and falsehood. An education which is too programmed, is based on fear. Fecundity, in contrast, is based on trust in life and in the source of all life.

It is essential for all human beings to discover and to live their fecundity. Through this they will penetrate into the heart of God, into the heart of divine fecundity who is the Holy Spirit.

All human beings long to continue beyond death. They hope that at their death they will not simply leave an empty bed in a hospital or in their homes, but that they will continue to live somewhere, that their memory, their life, their spirit will be perpetuated. Thus they will live in those to whom they have given life, in those whose hearts they have awakened and opened to a greater love, and in those to whom they have communicated the mystery of God.

Human beings' awareness of their fecundity allows them in part to overcome the fear of death. Fecundity consists of the gift which contributes to the fullness of the physical, spiritual and divine life of another, to the joy in living and existing, and growing to fulfilment. The awareness of our fecundity is to know that one day someone will look at us and say: 'You are one of the reasons why I am alive and happy'. It is the joy of knowing that we, too, are able to cry out to so many others: 'Thank you! If I am alive and if I am happy, it is thanks to you!' Fecundity is to know that we are all interdependent and that we are able to communicate life to others: our love, our trust, our hope, our faith, our joy and our peace. Someone closed up and moody will not give life to those around him, on the contrary he can make them closed up and moody. Fear can be contagious. Fear gives birth to fear, aggression to aggression. Tenderness engenders tenderness; confidence engenders confidence, and kindness, kindness. I love that phrase that Abbé Pierre, founder of the international Emmaus communities, says so often: 'We need to be contagious with hope.'

Yet, some people seem to be deeply blocked inside. They live in their heads. Life does not flow harmoniously within them. It is as if they were cut off from the world of their own feelings and this cuts them off from an aspect of reality. They can be productive or gifted intellectually, but they do not give life. They are not able to listen to others, to sense their sufferings and needs, to relax with them. To be fruitful they need to find an inner wholeness and harmony, and be in touch with the source of their being and the world of their deepest feelings. They will have to re-enter in a painful way into the anguish which was unbearable during child-hood and which they have hidden behind inner walls or blocks. This can will be done if they are accompanied by someone who is compassionate, competent, and committed to them.

Fruitfulness and Celibacy

Loving parents are able to discover and live their fecundity. They have the joy of being called 'Daddy' and 'Mummy'. It is difficult for men and women who have known rejection, and have felt they were a disappointment and a burden to their parents, to discover their fruitfulness. No one has ever revealed to them their capacity to give life and be fruitful. Instead, they have been made to feel that they were a nuisance for others, and even that they brought anguish and death instead of life. They have been separated from the family milieu. Those who have been so deeply rejected sense that life has no meaning, since they have nothing to bring to others.

When people are unable to marry, or have the feeling 'no one wants me', they can suffer from a certain sense of sterility which convinces them that they are not a source of life for others. This is the case with Georgette, of whom I spoke in chapter 1, who said 'I will never be able to marry because my mother said that if I married, I might have a child like me.' This is the hidden message in a forced abortion: 'Your fruit is rotten. The tree (which is you) is also rotten.' If we impose on young people situations in which they cannot be fruitful, we imply that they are no good and that their fruit will not be good.

If someone is not able to have a child, then we must help that person to discover how he or she is able to be fruitful, to give life and hope to others in another way.

The fundamental question, at l'Arche, for those who are not able to establish a family, is how to help them find meaning in their lives and true fecundity. Without this, their bodies will always cry out their need to give life and their hearts will live with a sense of sterility. They will seek to appease the anguish of isolation through pleasure and distractions. If, however, they discover their human and spiritual fecundity, their bodies will no longer hunger in the same way. The role of l'Arche, and of all those who are close to people with intellectual disabilities, is to help them to discover that their life has meaning, that the community, the Church, society needs them and that they have a special capacity to touch hearts and to give life.

Many of us at l'Arche, and many of those who are near to people with disabilities, have lived through this experience. We have discovered how our own hearts have been awakened by them. We have experienced a profound healing coming from their trust, their spontaneity, their love and their simple affection.

A short time ago, a Jesuit priest sent a very competent, but anguished man to a l'Arche community in Canada. Later the priest told me: 'The unconditional welcome by the people of the community so staggered him that, after a year, he returned a changed man. He still has his anguish, but he has learnt to accept it better.' Being transformed doesn't always mean being healed of all anguish, but the person can now live with it. It can now have a place in all that defines who they are. They are of the stars, but also of the earth. Life is not just a question of either being whole or being in need of healing. It is discovering that our fecundity is not extinguished by our wounds or by our needing to be healed. This is one example among thousands of people who have been healed and transformed by those with disabilities at the heart of our communities.

However, to be fruitful requires two people. No one can be fruitful alone. It is the reality of the seed and the earth, of the man and the woman. Biological fecundity demands that there be two.

It is the same with spiritual fecundity. A child grows harmoniously when he feels loved by two people, drawn into the circle, of love which flows between the father and the mother.[1] In the Christian vision of sexuality, man and woman render present the mystery of the Trinity. Our God is not a solitary God, but one God in three Persons. In fecundity, there is also a trinitarian mystery.

The Fruitfulness of the Community

If it is true that, in order to be fruitful, it is necessary to be two, we must ask ourselves what is the fecundity of the community in which people with disabilities live? First of all, many people with developmental disabilities have an amazing capacity to create community life, a capacity that people more developed intellectually do not usually have. At l'Arche, we have often been astonished to hear the reflections of visitors: 'It does me so much good to be with you. Living continually in the big city, I am constantly under pressure; I have to create barriers to protect myself. Here, for the first time, I feel liberated because I am so welcomed.'

In spite of having been abandoned as children and socially excluded most of their lives, many people with developmental disabilities have an astounding capacity of relationship on the level of the heart. They truly fit the definition of the 'wounded healer'. They do not live in the world of ideas and theories. They are down-to-earth and do not try to defend their position, their place in the social scale. Often they live outside the conventions of social politeness. They do not look at visitors in terms of their qualifications or what they do. They are drawn to the heart, to the person who exists behind the mask. It is because they have this capacity to live close to the values of the heart that they find their place in the community. They respond to love. They know how to celebrate, to live joyfully, while people who are more intellectual and more normally self-assured are often ill at ease.

Recently a Canadian, who had been an assistant in l'Arche fourteen years earlier, came back to see us. I had completely forgotten him. It was Alfred who threw himself into his arms, remembered his name, and where he had worked. The former assistant was very touched. The men and women at the heart of our communities have an amazing capacity for welcome. They give life and warmth; they know how to recognise another person and his or her needs.

At l'Arche, we often make pilgrimages and journeys in small groups. Everywhere we are welcomed, and we are surprised by the remarks: 'There is something in your group which is so simple and glowing that we are warmed and comforted by it.'

At Easter 1981, there was an international 'Faith and Light' pilgrimage to Lourdes. We were about 12,000 pilgrims: 4,000 young people and friends, 4,000 people with disabilities and 4,000 parents, representing 350 communities of 'Faith and Light' across the world. It was an explosion of joy. On Easter Sunday in the afternoon, there was a great celebration on the Basilica Esplanade. From all corners of the city, the communities paraded to the meeting. Everyone wore a poncho – of different colours and different styles. It was the great celebration of the poor and the weak. They came, some in wheelchairs, some walking with difficulty, some very disfigured; but all, or nearly all, smiling, cheering and shouting with joy.

The next morning a television cameraman asked me: 'How do you explain all this? I like my job, I have money, but they have something I don't have. They have joy.' I responded by quoting from the Gospel: 'The stone which the builders rejected has become the cornerstone.' If people with disabilities are accepted as they are, they can become the heart of the community, and of society. They can renew the community by their simplicity and their trust, easing tensions and bringing down barriers. Human beings, instead of being rivals, are then able to co-operate so that those who are the most poor can grow and truly take their place in the world.

The Taizé Brothers living in Bangladesh helped to organise a pilgrimage for people with disabilities and others coming from different faith traditions. They wrote in a letter:

We discover more and more that those who are rejected by society because of their weakness and their apparent uselessness are in fact a presence of God. If we welcome them, they lead us progressively out of a world of competition and the need to do great things, towards a world of communion of hearts, a life that is simple and joyful, where we do small things with love.

The challenge today in our country urges us on to show that the service of our weak and vulnerable brothers and sisters means opening a way of peace and unity: welcoming each other in the rich diversity of religions and cultures, serving the poor together, preparing a future of peace.[2]

When people with a disability find meaning to their lives, through and in a truly loving community, they become fruitful. They are no longer 'disabled,' but just people amongst others in the community, having their own unique gift which others do not have. Then there is no longer any need for jealousy. Each one has found his or her place. The difference between people is no longer a threat, a source of envy, jealousy or rivalry, but has become rather a source of richness. Together we constitute a 'body', open and welcoming where we can be ourselves.

It is of course necessary at the same time to help those with a disability to progress, to develop to the maximum their potential for autonomy, for work, for service. Never should we, under the pretext that they have a unique gift of the heart, impede the development of their latent abilities.

In order for people in our communities to discover their fruitfulness in the community, they have to find others who want to live with them and are willing to let themselves be touched in the depths of their hearts by them. The presence of friends and visitors is also important, if they have learnt to lower barriers built around their hearts.

In some institutions and group homes I have visited, there is something of a gulf between the staff and the people with disabilities. The latter are not really being helped to discover their true fecundity, because of the lack of hope in those around them. The staff looks after them but often do not seem to believe in their fecundity. Sometimes they even hinder it. They find it more convenient just to plant them in front of the television. They do not encourage them to exercise their gifts, their capacities of welcome and for relationship, because there is no one to welcome. Sometimes they encourage sexual relations amongst them, but they refuse them biological fecundity and have no concern for their human and spiritual fecundity.

Spiritual Fecundity

The spiritual fecundity of people with disabilities who live in a community of faith grows even more when they have a personal experience of God. I am astonished by their capacity for faith, whether they are Muslims, Hindus, Jews or Christians. Their openness to God touches me deeply. They have a capacity for trust that surpasses most of us who are considered 'normal'. Some live with the same trust we find in children and which is sometimes destroyed in a more sophisticated person, who has become cynical. Those with intellectual disabilities often find it hard to verbalise what goes on within them, but many seem to enjoy a tranquillity and an inner peace at prayer time or during the liturgy, or after communion. Some who have severe disabilities sometimes experience moments of serenity during liturgical celebrations although at other times they are constantly agitated. They seem to be living something true and profound within them. Perhaps they are discovering their interior beauty, finding their true place in the heart of the Church and the universe, in the Heart of God. Through this personal experience of God which is given to them they can discover their true identity. Such an experience often remains hidden from those who are more intellectual, or overactive, or overly concerned about their status in society.

A few years ago, Yolanda entered into a phase of profound regression. She is an intelligent, but deeply broken, young woman. Rejected by her family, considered as 'abnormal', she was put into an institution and sterilised. She had made several attempts at suicide and had a terribly wounded image of herself and her femininity. She regressed to the point of being like a small child, needing the most elementary care for several weeks. Someone had to be constantly with her. One day, Father Thomas came to give her communion; he prayed with her and whispered something into her ear. For the first time, Yolanda opened her eyes and smiled. It seemed that this was a moment of breakthrough, the beginning of her return to life. Father Thomas had simply told her that he needed her and her prayer, the offering of her suffering. She sensed this to be true, that he did need her, that she was able to help him bring life to others.

When human beings discover that they are truly loved by God and that they can live a relationship with God, a change takes place within them. They are no longer disheartened by their limits and disabilities. By this union with Jesus, they can communicate life. They are able to believe the words of Jesus: 'Everything you ask of the Father in my name, I will give it to you.'

I am struck by the way in which the men in my own home pray for countries at war and for other areas of pain in the world. They truly believe that through prayer they are able to affect a situation in the world.

So many of the men and women in our homes have compassionate hearts and an intuition of other people's pain. I think of Joan, who herself has suffered much. She is hemiplegic, and has a poor and awkward body. She would so love to be married and to have children. One day, she sensed that I was feeling very tired and came close to me, put her hand on my head with tenderness and said to me: 'I love you, you know.' At that moment, I felt like a little child. She knew how to warm my heart and to give me life. So many in l'Arche are deeply happy when they can do something for an elderly person or someone even more disabled than themselves. They love to take little children into their arms! Of course, they can be awkward and sometimes they make the little children cry. But their hearts are so delicate. They want to help so much ... It is important for a community like ours, to enable people to assume a responsibility however small for someone weaker.

Difficulties

It is not simple to find one's true fecundity. Many who have an intellectual disability remain frustrated and dissatisfied. They want to be like their brothers and sisters who are married. Some want to go on living with their parents or live independently. They have a hard time accepting their fragility and their hearts can be filled with anger. Some have closed themselves up in a role which is not their real self. Others are torn between the demands of society, with its ambivalent values, and their own human, psychic, and spiritual reality, with all its limits and wounds. The fecundity of these people is ignored by the world and by themselves. They do not know how to give life through their hearts and their love. Naturally they feel frustrated.

It is not surprising then that so many people with mild learning disabilities or emotional disturbances are torn between the attraction of 'productivity', with the esteem, the riches, the feelings of superiority that this can bring, and their true fecundity. They do not dare to believe that, in spite of their limits, they can be fruitful and give life. The mass media confirms their doubts and pulls them towards a competitive and aggressive world where they are not at ease. It is not surprising that they are confused.

Communities are called to dialogue with them, carrying their confusion, helping them to grow through their aggression and their frustrations, hoping against hope for the day when they will be able to go beyond the illusory desire for 'normality' to the peace which comes from the profound acceptance of oneself and of others. Community life gives each one the possibility of living encounters with others and with God. Only when one has accepted one's fragility in a realistic way can it be possible to overcome it. Some can then assume greater responsibility in the community or even hope realistically of one day finding someone they can marry.

The Fruitfulness of Suffering

Community must also teach us how to live with those who do not attain this peace and acceptance of themselves. It is my faith in Jesus, in his sufferings and his resurrection, which helps me, with others, to stay close to those who constantly live in pain and anguish, whose hearts are wounded and broken, whose bodies are disfigured. These are people who have been torn apart by rejection, there is a void in them, filled sometimes by upsurges of aggression or strong sexual impulses. Nonetheless, they too are children of God. The community is called to carry them in faith and to offer, with them, their cries and their sufferings. I believe that there is a mysterious fecundity in suffering. It is difficult to speak of this, which flows from my faith. My belief is that those whose suffering is rejected by other human beings become as fertilising manure at the heart of the community: the excrement of animals and of humans is good for the earth. That which is rotten nourishes the earth and helps it to bear fruit, to give life. I believe that the sufferings of human beings and their poverty are like a cry which ascends to God; a cry that brings God down among us.

Isaiah says of the suffering servant:

> Without beauty, without majesty,
> no looks to attract our eyes;
> a thing despised and rejected by men,
> a man of sorrows and familiar with suffering,
> a man to make people screen their faces;
> he was despised and we took no account of him.
>
> (Isaiah 53:2–3)

These words can be applied to so many men and women in the world who suffer from rejection, sometimes from birth, sometimes even from conception. How can we understand and give meaning to this pain? Is there a link between the suffering we see in some people in our communities and the following words of Isaiah?

And yet ours were the sufferings he bore,
ours the sorrows he carried ...
Yet he was pierced through for our faults ...

(Isaiah 53:4–5)

People in pain are often totally unaware that their distress can bear fruit. Perhaps the community, in living with them and their cries, can offer this pain on their behalf to the Father in the belief that their cries are heard; that the Father makes them fruitful in union with the Passion of his Son.[3]

If we remain at the level of material things, searching only for productivity and possessions, death will appear as the most terrible event for a human being, the most radical break. If on the other hand we place ourselves at the level of fecundity, we can discover that death is a beginning. We can let go of life, for there are bonds with those we leave behind which remain forever. Death will then seem a little less terrifying as it is the return to the Father. In the Christian vision, death is the summit of gift and sacrifice: we give our lives for our friends, and in this we are fruitful.

The Celebration of Death

A community which knows how to celebrate life and fecundity must also know how to celebrate death. Freud, in *Our Attitude Towards Death*, takes the old Latin adage, 'If you want peace, prepare for war', and transposes it to, 'If you want to live life, prepare yourself for death'. If we live in fear of death, if we hide it from ourselves and others, we become anguished by the signs which announce it: sickness, disabilities, diminishing strength, setbacks, a sense that life is passing by. Death is part of the natural cycle. Certainly death, and particularly a brutal death, is a terrible reality; but, at the same time, it is a deeply natural reality, a reality written in our flesh, which so many others before us have lived through and beyond.

There can be an intimate link between an anguished sexuality and the fear of death. If a community knows how to celebrate death with realism and with tenderness, it will be able to assuage the fears of its members with regard to this fundamental reality. It is not a question of hiding from the ever-present reality of death, nor of 'prettifying' it, which would be another way of running away from it. It is a question of looking at it with serenity, of speaking about it, of praying and seeking to see it and to live it with the eyes of God. This does not mean a denial of its painful aspect. Grief is a profoundly human, psychological and spiritual reality.

The death of someone we love is always painful. To love is to carry another within us, to keep a special place in our heart for him or her. This spiritual space is nourished by a physical presence; death, then, tears out a part of our own heart and puts us in a place of loneliness. Those who deny the suffering of death have never truly loved; they live in a spiritual illusion. To celebrate death, then, is not to deny the pain and the grief it involves; it is to give space to live it, to speak about it, and even to sing of it. It is to give mutual support, looking the reality in the face and placing all in the Heart of God in deep trust. Jesus did not come to abolish suffering and death, but to show us the way to live them.

In l'Arche communities, we are often called to face the reality of death. We see both wrenching, cruel, accidental deaths, and sometimes gentler, predictable deaths, anticipated by sickness and failing strength.

There is a way of announcing a death to the community which brings peace. In our community we have a vigil of prayer where we speak together of the one who has just died and often show slides. Wherever possible we keep watch with the body and give an important place to the funeral mass. In November, the month when, traditionally, we commemorate those who have died, we share our memories of them, taking time to visit the graves of parents and to pray there. Hiding the reality of death is unhealthy and can create deep-seated fears. As we become freer to speak of our fears, we begin the process of liberation from them.

I remember Francis and Peter, two men with learning disabilities. Both had difficulty in walking. They went to keep watch with Frederick's body, an assistant who had died from cancer after a long illness and whom we had been able to keep in l'Arche during the last months of his life after the doctors could no longer do anything for him in the hospital. Francis was especially touched and said: 'He's beautiful! He's smiling. Can I kiss him?' He kissed Frederick on his forehead and then exclaimed: 'Oh, he is cold!' He chuckled quietly and as he left, he said to Peter: 'Mummy is going to be surprised when I tell her I kissed a dead person.'

When we realise that the refusal to accept our own disability is, in part, a refusal of our own death, we can recognise how far Francis and Peter had progressed on that day in the acceptance of their own profound disabilities, for they had approached death in a realistic, simple and peaceful way.

Fecundity and Sterilisation

Is there a link between sterilisation and death? I am deeply disturbed by the number of parents today who seek sterilisation for their child with a developmental disability. Isn't it a serious injustice to so mutilate someone, especially when it is done without even asking the person's permission?

Some time ago, in Canada, a mother came to see me. Her daughter was in an apartment where men and women lived together, and the mother came for my advice because she was afraid that there might be 'an accident'. She asked me: 'Shouldn't I have her sterilised?' She helped me to understand the suffering and confusion of so many parents. Not only do they live with the disappointment and pain of having a child with a learning disability, but also they are rarely helped or supported in dealing with all the consequences. So many parents today, without being overprotective, are justifiably concerned about the sexual permissiveness propagated in some countries, where individualism is so accentuated.

I know of staff members in some institutions who, on the grounds of furthering the well-being and liberation of people with disabilities, believe without question that it is right to encourage indiscriminate sexual relations, regularly handing out contraceptives and advocating abortion in the case of an 'accident'. Physical union comes to be considered as the normal expression of a relationship.

These permissive attitudes can have serious consequences because, instead of considering and developing the capacities for love, relationship and commitment in those with a disability, they risk to imprison them in the search for pleasure for themselves, which can isolate them even more.

When a mother learns that in her daughter's residence there is such sexual permissiveness, how can she protest, knowing that, as a parent, she often has in fact no real possibility of choosing an alternative?

One day, a mother told me that she had had her daughter sterilised because there was danger where they were living that her daughter might be abused. I had the impression that, for the mother, the most terrible thing that could happen would be for her daughter to conceive a child. She did not seem concerned about, or even aware of, the terrible trauma her daughter might suffer if she was raped. If there was a real danger, should she not think rather of moving to another area or, at least, of seeing that her daughter was always accompanied? She should not leave her alone in the face of such a danger.

It is true, of course, that there are some mothers who are overly concerned about sexuality, for their daughters in particular, and who are unable to trust even the best team of educators.

What a responsibility for the Christian community! There are so few places today which welcome people for long periods, in the spirit of the Gospels, and which wish to help the person with a disability to develop their real fruitfulness. Why don't Christians react by creating more communities, where the poorest and the weakest are welcomed and respected in their deepest convictions?

It is important that the Church reminds us of the basic principles of life and of fecundity. But she must also insist that the men, women and children who have been put aside and looked down upon because of their fragility be welcomed into the Christian community, whatever form that may take. Only when such persons are truly loved as they are, can their broken affectivity be gradually healed. Only then can they become more mature and have a more developed sense of the needs of others.

How can families give support to other families that are in distress? During a retreat, a couple came to see me; the wife was pregnant. Twelve doctors had each diagnosed a high probability that the brain of the child would be profoundly damaged. All twelve had advised them to have an abortion. Some even told them that it was their duty to have an abortion rather than bring into the world a little boy who would suffer all his life and would cause suffering to future brothers and sisters. They asked my opinion. I told them that I could not accept the idea of killing a child, even a sick one. I promised them, rather vaguely, that I would help them if the child was born with a disability. Later they met the priest who was responsible for the retreat house who told the couple: 'If your baby is disabled and if you are unable to keep him, I will take him into my community and we will take care of him.' With that assurance, the mother decided not to have an abortion. Some months later, she gave birth to twins, both perfectly healthy.

Many families today are locked up in prisons of individualism and egoism. They refuse to open their homes and to welcome others. They are shut up in themselves. Sometimes they do not even want their own children. They see them as a disturbance to their material happiness. These families stifle their own fecundity, remain enclosed in sadness and hinder the fruitfulness of others. Is a renewal possible?

I believe that there is a profound bond between the love of the couple and fecundity. True love is necessarily fruitful, through the children of the couple or through the love and life the couple bring to others. Above all, the Church exalts human love; it believes profoundly in the beauty of sexual relationships. There is something deeply sacred and mysterious in the love of a husband and a wife, so sacred that this love is celebrated in a book of Scripture inspired by the Holy Spirit, the Song of Songs. That love is the sign and the image of the love of God.

However, that love was not given to enclose man and woman in a ghetto. It was given to open one to the other, to God, to others; to open the couple first of all to their own children; the fruit of their love and then to others, other families in need of help.

The relationship between man and woman is obviously different from those between male and female animals. Between man and woman there is friendship which precedes and follows the sexual relation and then the child needs during long years the loving presence of the two parents. The love between spouses can be expressed without any intention or natural possibility of conceiving a child. The woman, in fact, is fertile for only a few days each month and only up to a certain age. The hearts and bodies of the man and the woman are made in such a way that they are able to show love without biological fecundity. However, their union must always further a spiritual and human fecundity and bring to birth a greater love in the hearts of one for the other, for the children, and for those for whom they are responsible. The knowledge of the rhythms of fertility can oblige the man and the woman to bear these times of waiting. The union of their bodies is so sacred that it demands a readiness to wait and a degree of preparation which can sometimes be difficult.

The Church perceives the sacred aspect of this union of bodies in tenderness and it senses the gravity of artificial manipulation of fertility which can lead to the desecration of this love and thus to its death and can alter the natural functions of the organs of fecundity, which play their role in opening people to one another. Man and woman are called to live the mystery of the Trinity through their love for each other, through their fidelity to one another and through their fruitfulness.

Chapter Nine

A CELEBRATION OF UNITY

The Meaning of Pleasure

Today people talk a lot about 'the right to pleasure' and 'the right for autonomy' for those with disabilities; there is less said of their 'right to be loved and respected' in the totality of their being, and their 'right to have a fruitful and meaningful life'.

Aristotle defined pleasure as that which accompanies an activity exercised without interference. There is the pleasure of work, the pleasure of eating, the pleasure of singing. Each activity engenders its own pleasure. When we do something well, we become more aware of *being*, of *being alive*. The more an activity is good and well done, the more intense the pleasure which accompanies it. In order for human beings to be fully happy, they need to be able to develop their capacities to the maximum and to exercise their activities without hindrance.

It is difficult to learn how to play the piano, but when one does it is usually with pleasure. Psychologists often define pleasure as the result of fulfilled or satisfied desires. This implies that a person who is unable to exercise even the least activity in an appropriate way is in a state of sadness, of emptiness, and of anguish.

Without pleasure, or at least, without activity, we die; we fall into a form of depression, of 'non life'. The energies of life no longer flow forth in us; they turn in upon themselves. This is anguish. Energy, when it is no longer constructive and creative, becomes destructive.

If people come to l'Arche not knowing how to work or not wanting to work, and if they are disturbed and have difficulties at home, then they will seek satisfaction where they can, maybe through food or masturbation. Some people can take pleasure and a sense that they exist in negative attitudes; opposing and provoking others. Children who do not receive loving attention will seek an aggressive attention; they would rather receive blows than remain lonely and forgotten. Some people masturbate because it is their only moment of pleasure. Alone, in bed, they can at last feel some pleasure.

In some hospitals, asylums or residences, if the food is bad, or if there is no work (or, if it exists, is tedious or badly paid), or if the leisure activities are indifferent, then people will experience a terrible boredom, a lack of life. To escape from this many will seek sexual pleasures alone or with others. There is nothing else for them to do; they seek pleasure where they can find it.

The tragedy is that sexuality outside a relationship, outside a true bond of friendship, becomes a delusion. It loses its life-giving energy, its fecundity, its power to unite two human beings and deepen their love for one another. Instead, it becomes a pleasure which lasts only a fleeting moment, and after that moment there is nothing, no longer any relationship … nothing. One finds oneself alone, empty and in anguish.

In the past, masturbation was rigidly condemned. This condemnation led to fear, which nourished guilt and led to inhibitions, even hatred of oneself and one's body. Today, there is a tendency to say that masturbation is not serious, that we should let people do what they want, and that it is normal for an adolescent. It seems to me that the truth is somewhere between these two attitudes of rigidity and permissiveness. We should not condemn young people who masturbate. They have compulsions which they do not understand and are not yet able to control or integrate. However, it is important to help them find other activities where their energies can be fulfilled in a positive way. Masturbation can close them in on themselves, in a world of dreams and fantasies and prevent them from entering into true, loving relationships.

Pleasure is an ambiguous reality. There are dangerous pleasures, deadly pleasures, and those which create an addiction, a need, a habit; drugs, for example, not only imprison the person in a habit but also in an 'artificially induced pleasure' rather than 'of imaginary excitement'. The physical effect of drugs, the pleasure of the 'high' is very real, not imaginary. But the chemical pleasure is artificial and has the effect of distancing us from reality and from others. At the same time, such pleasures can be destructive and impede real growth. They can close people up in the virtual and the imaginary and keep them from knowing reality, from knowing their real needs and the needs of others and keeping them from loving other people and making an effort in the struggle for peace and justice. The pursuit of pleasure for oneself implies a certain indifference towards others; and, when the seeking becomes total, it cuts a person off from others. Beside the injustice created by those who oppress and torture the weak, there is also the injustice of those who are closed in on themselves, in their world of pleasure, refusing to share and communicate with others.

The pursuit of egotistical sexual pleasure can become like a drug, which prevents the heart from becoming sensitive to the needs and sufferings of others. It can enclose people within themselves, within their own feelings and subjective emotions, and cut them off from reality.

Pleasure, then, can be destructive; it can shut a person up in a world of isolation which can intensify the anguish, an anguish which makes the person seek other pleasures and compensations. It becomes then a vicious circle. The need for drugs and alcohol becomes greater as the person craves for more and more pleasure, because the anguish and inner pain become greater. This search is endless and leads eventually to death: a human being is never satisfied and always wants more. This dependence, which springs from anguish, takes flesh in the body, in the blood and creates a physical dependence.

For the rich, there is always a danger of letting oneself be seduced by the attraction of instant pleasure which can be bought. In rich families, every material need and desire of the child can be immediately satisfied, and eventually the child becomes spoiled. The word 'spoiled' is significant.

We all have to learn about our very human desires and impulses. Understanding our humanity means accepting that we have certain never ending desires that we do not need to say yes to. The pathway to maturity is learning to say no to those desires and impulses that we know will not lead to life, to deepening in our capacity to love ourselves and others. This education requires an inner strength, but it leads to hope and to wholeness, to open ourselves up to higher and more universal realities in the world of art, of knowledge and of religion.

The Discovery of True Joy

There are joys which open us to others and in some way strengthen us inwardly; they give us security and trust in ourselves, which in turn enable us to comprehend better our own real needs and those of others and to respond to them.

These joys are a nourishment and a resource which relax us and, at the same time, give us energy to continue the struggle against all those forces which enclose us in the prison of individualism, self-centredness and fear. They lead us along the way of love. When pleasure is taken as an end in itself, as an absolute, we withdraw within ourselves. When it is taken as nourishment and as an added gift, it opens us up to others. Pleasure is then no longer a wall preventing us from seeing others; it becomes a 'go-between', just as parents are go-betweens, allowing the child to be integrated in the universe; without this intermediary, the little one is afraid, closes up in isolation, becomes aggressive in self-defence. Through the presence of an intermediary, fear disappears and the child finds the confidence necessary to go towards others and to make friends with them, to love them and to co-operate with them. So it is with pleasure in its most beautiful form.

The bonds of mutual attraction between a man and woman can be very fulfilling and authentic. With, and in these bonds, the man and woman can be intermediaries to one another, giving each other security, opening each other up to others and to the universe. But also, this attraction can close the man and woman in on themselves in a form of fusion, each one upon and with the other. This hinders their harmonious and constructive integration into different places of belonging (the town, the parish, etc.) and into society at large.

Education consists in more than simply forbidding false pleasures; rather, it is to help people discover those sources of pleasure which bring. a deeper sense of fulfilment and, at the same time, give security, peace and confidence. The difficulty on the educational level is to know when to let a person discover by experience that certain pleasures are illusions and destructive, and when it is better simply to forbid the experience – hoping to prevent bad habits before they become rooted, but possibly arousing frustration and anger which can augment the desire. There are so many different situations, each of which need to be discerned with both delicacy and authority, that it is impossible to lay down precise guidelines. The important thing is to try to discover which attitudes allow a person to grow humanly and spiritually.

The Search for Sexual Relations in the Absence of Community and Celebration

It seems that in the culture of certain countries there is a link between the expression of genital sexuality and the disappearance of community life and the bonds of true friendship. The values of our society push people towards autonomy and individualism. To be strong is to have no need of another; to be free is to be dependent on no one. These are ideals which oppose that of community based on the acknowledgement of our gifts, our weaknesses, our need of others and our desire to grow in greater inner freedom. There is no longer, or at least much less of, a sense of sharing. Towns or villages tend to lose their soul and their sense of celebration, even though there is an increasing need and desire to celebrate together. In big cities, people are isolated, barricaded within their own four walls. Large or extended families, including uncles, aunts, grandparents, cousins, have disappeared. Even the nuclear family is in danger because man and woman are too often so busy and stressed; they no longer communicate and celebrate together. People find themselves isolated and anguished, often lacking inner strength. Therefore, they seek excitement in violent or erotic films, or in alcohol or parties. They throw themselves into the pursuit of political and other causes, in hyperactivity, without sufficient reflection. Or they seek strong emotions in transitory, egotistical sexual relations without any real intimacy of the heart and without covenant. In all these situations they risk losing themselves.

Forbidding genital sexuality outside marriage will never really remedy the situation. What is needed is the creation of communities where people love each other and where there is sharing and mutual commitment in an authentic relationship which is celebrated with joy, enthusiasm and creativity. A world without joy and celebrations of this kind will necessarily engender superficial sexuality. When sexual relations between a man and a woman involve neither love nor celebration, when they are not the sign and fruit of a mutual commitment, they cannot bring true joy and the deep pleasure that strengthens the bond between them. They are rather the fruit of anguish and come from the fear of isolation.

People with Intellectual Disabilities Have a Capacity for Celebration

One of the things that strikes me most about those who have an intellectual disability is their capacity for celebration. One might say that it is one of the basic characteristics of the communities of l'Arche and of Faith and Light. But, I notice this same phenomenon wherever there are people with intellectual disabilities. Most of them are not all concerned about 'what others think'. They love to fool around, to clap their hands, to play, to laugh and to dance, while people who are more rational and conventional tend to be more stiff, tense, unable to smile or even sing. In l'Arche and Faith and Light, when we mime scenes from the Gospels, the assistants are sometimes a too self-conscious and nervous to play the part of

Jesus. Our people are more relaxed, freer and less concerned about what others think.

There is much enthusiasm in some countries for the 'normalisation' of those with disabilities. This is excellent if, by normalisation, we mean the exercise of the fundamental rights of all human beings: the right to have work, to use public transport and the public swimming pool, etc. But it is important not to confuse conformity with the respect of difference. It is important to respect the culture and the special needs and gifts of those with a learning disability. They will never be intellectuals; they will not be able to appreciate things that are too intellectual and rational; they are more intuitive and less verbal. Their culture and their own needs and their gifts are more in the realm of affectivity. That is why they love celebrations in which they can actively participate.

Our modern culture no longer knows how to celebrate. It knows about 'parties' where one drinks, eats, laughs and meets others. It knows about leisure activities: television, shows, sport, dances, games, books, etc. It knows about holidays when one does what one wants; but it does not know what celebration is.

Celebration is a cry of joy, an acknowledgement that our lives are woven together; it is the joyful recognition that we are bonded together with one another as part of the same body, that our differences are a treasure and a richness, and that we can let down the barriers which keep us from one another. We rejoice at being able to share what is most profound and most vulnerable within us: we are bonded together in trust.

Celebration is a reality of community, springing from the union and communion between its members. Its purpose is not to prove anything. It is simply the pinnacle of community life, an expression of unity which, at the same time, forges this unity.

Celebration involves the body and the senses; it involves music and song, our best clothes, flowers, beauty; it involves good food, perhaps some wine and fun, movement and dance, joy and humour, prayer and thanksgiving. Each human reality has its place in celebration. Celebration is a manifestation and a recalling of our deepest and most important values; it holds up and honours all those things in life that call us to unity and to love.

In l'Arche, we celebrate birthdays: a moment to express, through the festivities, that someone *is* a special gift for the community; we talk of his or her life and special qualities. It is a time to say simply why we are happy the person is with us, helping us to build community. The person celebrated is the centre of the feast. We choose the entertainment, the presents and the food according to their particular preferences, needs, sense of humour and expectations.

We celebrate religious feasts, Christmas, Easter and Pentecost — feasts which remind us how much God loves his people and how close God is to us today. Humanity is not all alone amidst all the pain, inequalities and anguishes of our world. The community is not alone either: God is watching over it and leading it. Each person is in the hands of the Father, no one is alone.

We celebrate arrivals and departures. We celebrate those who have been with l'Arche for many years. We celebrate the end of the year by recalling all the events for which we give thanks. Every occasion is an opportunity for celebration.

When we celebrate, we sing together, laugh together, and pray together. This creates in the heart of each one a sense of belonging to the group, and to the community. We have been called together, called to live and work together, each one with his or her capacities, needs, gifts, and place. Among us there are bonds, a covenant, created by God. That covenant is not something which stifles or hinders personal growth. On the contrary, it confirms our growth and calls us to go further: it liberates; it is a call to greater inner freedom and responsibility. It is God who called us out of our isolation in order to live together; it is God who has chosen us and brought us to l'Arche to build community. God has given each one of us a gift which we are called to develop so that the body of community be beautiful.

Each group of men and women have their celebrations with its symbols, its language, its costumes which unify the members and give them a sense of belonging. Armed forces have parades (but this is not celebration!); African villages have their dances, their rituals and their ceremonies of initiation; clubs have their traditions and their 'liturgies'; psychoanalysts of different schools have their language and their symbols.

Depending on the structures and kinds of groupings, certain ways of celebrating can close the members in on themselves or open them to others. The sense of belonging and of fellowship can be exclusive or it can be open. Exclusiveness implies elitism; it can then become a show of power: we are the best, the strongest, the 'saved'. This is not true celebration which, on the contrary, is open to all. Openness implies humility and a certain admission of our poverty: no one is excluded; it is open to all. At the heart of the celebration is the presence of the weakest and the poorest people. A true celebration is one open to all those who recognise and wish to live the covenant, to celebrate it and give thanks.

At the heart of the Christian community is the celebration of the Eucharist the Supper of the Lord. At the heart of this feast is God who becomes small and poor, mysteriously present under the appearances of bread and wine. God comes to give himself to each one of us in our littleness and our poverty. The Eucharist is the celebration of the love of Jesus and of his resurrection. It announces his return; it is a sign of hope. But the Eucharist is also the presence of suffering. It is the supreme sacrifice of Jesus, where he gave his life; his blood is spilt, his body given. All the pain and brokenness of humanity is present there, as well as all our hope for love and joy. It is the sign of the fecundity of all suffering offered in union with Jesus, whose suffering saves and liberates.

The Eucharist is, *par excellence*, a celebration of unity, giving a sense of belonging to Jesus and to his body which is the Church, and to that cell of the Church which is our particular community. What is special in the Eucharist is that it is both a community celebration and a very intimate, personal reality. The Eucharist begins with the Word, community song and prayer; it ends in silence, a heart-to-heart relationship with Jesus, where each one eats his body and drinks his blood. It is a moment of communion: 'He who eats my body and drinks my blood lives in me and I in him.' The two become one in one flesh, the flesh of Christ. Other celebrations can give a sense of belonging but they do not always end in intimacy. They are not necessarily an experience of personal friendship with another. This is lived at other moments.

In many of our communities, the community members belong to different Christian traditions. We cannot always share the Eucharist together at the same table of the Lord. We are learning to find other ways of celebrating our unity prayerfully and hopefully. One of the important ways is to follow the example of Jesus who knelt down and washed the feet of his disciples; on important occasions we wash each others' feet, revealing our love for one another through this humble gesture of service.

The Eucharist and the washing of the feet are reminders that community is not an easy place, but a place of growth in the heart of God. They are a nourishment to help us walk along the road of love and liberation. They bind together, in a mysterious way, the pain and the joys of community, the covenant, a word of hope, an intimate communion with God and with one's brothers and sisters.

A community which no longer celebrates its joy at being together, united to God, and open to others, risks death. Rules and regulations do not give life. Such a community has lost its soul and becomes a skeleton. The heart of a community shows itself through the different forms of celebration and in the love, the mutual trust, the joy of being together, brothers and sisters, living and sharing the same goal.

Celebration, Aggression and Forgiveness

Celebration can liberate aggression, which is a wall that separates people. Aggression can be offensive and defensive. It protects and repulses. It is founded upon defence mechanisms. It hides that which is profound and most intimate in us, the vulnerability of our hearts, our longing to love and to be loved, our thirst for tenderness, for compassion and understanding, and for personal relationships. This aggression or hardness is the result of wounds, misunderstandings, injustices, and incomprehension, of guilt and of fear. Aggression divides; it is partisan; it creates blockages which can close people inside themselves; it separates; it causes tension. If it takes root, it destroys community.

There is a visible aggression which can be dangerous when it leads to division, to schism, and tears the community apart. But visible aggression can also be a signal that tells us something is wrong; and this can lead to dialogue and to forgiveness, which allows for growth in truth and the discovery of a new unity. In effect, there is a healthy aggression which is a cry for space, a cry for truth, a cry for recognition.

There is also a hidden, more passive aggression which is never openly expressed; it is a form of depression. People are too afraid of the manifestations of aggression, and of the diversities and the splits at the centre of the community. So, the members hide themselves from each other, speaking only of superficialities. There is no dialogue; subjects which risk bringing the discord to the surface are taboo. Conversation conforms to the rules of politeness, but fear and lack of mutual trust remain; there are impenetrable barriers between people. The aggression or depression is there, undermining true relationships; people are living in pretence; they may be living together but in fact are hiding from each other. In order to reach unity, we have to acknowledge consciously the division, the aggression, the fear which lives in our hearts; only then will we find the remedies and be able to come to dialogue and forgiveness.

There is a link between forgiveness and celebration. True celebration implies forgiveness and flows from it. When the prodigal son returned home after a debauched life, the father forgave him and gathered everyone together for a feast. He said to his servants: 'Hurry up! Bring the most beautiful robe and put it on him. Place a ring on his finger and shoes on his feet. Bring the fatted calf, kill it, we will eat and celebrate because my son who was dead has returned to life. He was lost and he is found! Let us celebrate!' (Luke 15: 22–4)

Some people would like community celebrations to be spontaneous; they say they can celebrate only if they feel like it.

However, if we waited until everyone spontaneously felt like celebrating, there would not be very many celebrations! Between a rigid ritual and a spontaneous manifestation, there is a middle road. Celebrations need to be prepared. It is important to plan the songs, and the order of the various activities, but at the same time remaining flexible and able to change: to prolong certain moments of fun, joy or of grace and times of silence, or to cut things short if necessary. It is often the unexpected and the spontaneous which nourish most.

Many of those with disabilities need to be stimulated and called into activities. This can require energy. It could be so much easier just to put them in front of the television, or a show that others perform, or simply let them do their own thing. Once they are called to the celebration, they become the heart of it, and draw others into it, creating a warmth and special joy.

The Celebration of Unity

The joy which flows from the physical union of intimacy, when it is true, is the joy of love, the joy of knowing that one is not alone on the road of our earthly pilgrimage. Physical intimacy is the summit of this kind of friendship which also implies daily companionship. The joy of the wedding feast is the joy of unity. The book of Genesis and the Gospel speak of man and woman called to become one flesh. The word, 'flesh', as used here, does not simply signify a physical reality or, still less, that flesh is opposed to spirit. It means the profound unity of two persons, who become a sign of the presence of the Holy Trinity. In John's gospel (ch. 17), Jesus prayed that his disciples might be *one* as the Father and he are *one*. It is impossible not to connect the two texts, especially since St Paul, in his epistle to the Ephesians, compares the union of the Church with Jesus, to the union between man and woman in love.

When the two spouses give themselves to each other in complete trust, in total gift, and in great tenderness, it is a celebration of unity. It is not simply a celebration of the love between the spouses, but also of the unity between the parents and their children. It seals the unity of the family and its vocation to love and to service.

John Paul II commented on the text from Genesis (2:23–5) where man meets woman for the first time, 'This at last is bone of my bones and flesh of my flesh. She shall be called Woman because she is taken out of Man.' The text continues: 'Therefore, a man leaves his father and his mother and cleaves to his wife, and they become one flesh. And the man and his wife were both naked and were not ashamed.' Pope John Paul II says that this text announces the first celebration of humanity with an experience of the spiritual significance of the body.[1]

Isn't the search for unity the great search of human beings; unity within their own selves and with others, unity with the cosmos, and unity with God? The deepest cry of the unconscious is to find our lost unity. Before birth, the infant is not conscious of the unity it has with its mother or the way in which his or her personality is being formed by this unity (or sometimes by the lack of it). But, from the time the baby leaves the security, the peace and the harmony of its mother's womb, it is in search of another unity. The union of spouses is one of the major experiences of that search for the lost unity, but it is attained only if the two persons consciously give themselves one to the other.

The unity which is celebrated by the two spouses is not, first of all, a physical unity, the union of their bodies. The physical union is an expression of a union that already exists. It is the unity of being one heart, one soul, one spirit. Man and woman, profoundly different in some aspects, each one fully him or herself, with their gifts and temperaments, are companions for life, special friends united in tenderness, in their vision of the world and in their love of God. The spousal union is a profound unity, a sign of other unities. But it is not the only unity; there are others. If those who cannot marry, or are not called to marry, do not find ways to celebrate unity in other forms, their hearts and their bodies will cry out; the physical and biological need of sexuality will cry out and seek ways of fulfilment other than in committed friendships.

This is why celebrations at l'Arche have a very deep meaning. If a home or community forgets these celebrations, in all probability, there will be a tendency to sexual immaturity among its members. Community celebrations are called to be celebrations of unity.

Happiness

The human being thirsts for happiness. Those who have the impression that they will never be happy enter into the process of emotional death. They find themselves alone, faced with their limits, and their poverty; they succumb to sadness and despair. Despair is life which turns in against itself. When life does not flow outwards and bear fruit, it tends to destroy itself.

Throughout the ages, one of the great symbols of the happiness sought by each human being is that of the wedding feast. This symbol of unity is so powerful that the mass media uses it in order to sell all kinds of products: in order to be loved, to find a partner, you must wear such and such a garment, use such and such a perfume, be seen eating such and such a cheese! This symbol is also the *leitmotiv* for art, for films, and for songs. Humanity is always searching for that unchanging love which will take away all loneliness, all pain, all suffering, all division, all war.

The final goal of humankind, to which we all aspire, is that unity where there will be no more struggle and warfare. Struggle implies the possibility of being vanquished and oppressed, and thus to be isolated. The wedding feast is the final goal of all struggle since it is the celebration of love and unity.

The quest for unity is deeply rooted in humanity. It is inscribed in all the great religions and, in particular, in the Judeo-Christian tradition, where it is said that at the end of time there will be one people, one nation, one city, the heavenly Jerusalem, where there will be no more war. To express this unity of the people of God, Scripture uses the symbols of the wedding feast. In the Book of Revelation, John sees a new heaven and a new earth:

I saw the holy city, and the new Jerusalem, coming down from God out of heaven, as beautiful as a bride all dressed for her husband. Then I heard a loud voice call from the throne, 'You see this city. Here God lives among men. He will make his home among them; they shall be his people, and he will be their God; his name is God-with-them. He will wipe away all tears from their eyes; there will be no more death, and no more mourning or sadness. The world of the past has gone. (Revelation 21:1–4)

The Kingdom of God is like a celebration of love, 'a wedding feast' (Matthew 22:1–10), a celebration of unity.

People with learning disabilities, like all human beings, yearn for this celebration of unity. It is their deepest yearning. And that celebration of love is something which flows from the whole being.

But how can this unity of love be celebrated? That is a fundamental question for all of us. In order to celebrate this unity, we must be liberated from our egoism and hardness, and go beyond ourselves, opening up to others. If we remain imprisoned in the search to satisfy our own needs, we can only celebrate our own acquisitions and possessions; we cannot celebrate love and unity.

To celebrate unity is to discover the unity that people have among themselves. Paul in his epistle, compares the Church to a body in which each person, with his own gifts, is a member (1 Corinthians 12). Human beings, united by Christ, become a single body, a single spirit. No longer are they rivals, living in competition. No longer do they see differences as a threat, but as a treasure. They live in harmony with each other; they no longer need to attack each other but, on the contrary, they need each other with their different gifts. When we discover the riches of interdependence, we are no longer alone; we are together, helping one another, each one with his or her differences and gifts. Only then can that which is most profound in each one be awakened, bringing new life to the vulnerable hearts, often hidden behind walls of aggression and defence, but capable of welcoming God and others without losing what is most precious in self: one's liberty, one's deepest identity, one's love.

There is nothing more beautiful on earth than people who have trust in each other. The work of God is all that fosters the growth of trust. The work of the evil spirit is all that separates: breakdown of relationship between people, lack of trust, and doubt.

The celebration of unity is the celebration of the trust we have in each other. Yet, our hearts remain wounded. In each of us there is sin, darkness and evil; we are not yet in heaven. Celebrations on earth are essentially celebrations of hope. Such hope does not deceive, because it is founded on our trust in Jesus who has conquered death and evil. It is he who calls us to live a covenant of love with him and asks us to invite others to live it with us.

CONCLUSION

Community is a place where people can grow towards wholeness, particularly in the area of their affectivity and their sexuality. Each one can gradually move toward the integration of his or her sexual instincts through authentic relationships which touch and call forth each one in their most intimate self. This transpires through a sense of belonging, through a personal and communal fruitfulness, through celebrations and, above all, through a life in communion with Jesus. However, community life implies that each day each one of us says anew 'Yes' to our own growth. If community is a place of healing relationships, it is also a place of struggle and inner pain. When we live alone, we can easily believe that we are whole and holy; when we live with others we see that we are not. We discover quickly, in the depths of ourselves, areas of hate and anguish, of jealousy and fear, of blockages and the need to dominate or to prove one's worth.

Human life is never static. It is either deepening and continually opening up gently towards reality and truth, or else it is angry with reality, withdrawing and regressing into itself. Human beings either open themselves more and more in freedom and trust or else they close themselves up behind barriers of fear or anger. A community can only be a place of healing and growth if it remains dynamic in love and hope. Communities can become soulless institutions, administrations, 'hierarchies', places where the rules and organisation are more important than communion and friendship among its members. A community needs to be constantly nourished and revitalised, otherwise it risks closing in on itself. Then it is no longer a community.

That is precisely the challenge of l'Arche and Faith and Light. Each one of our communities has experienced the forces of despair which spring from inside or outside the community and which stifle life; each has experienced also the forces of hope which give life. To live in community is a struggle against the forces of despair. There are however certain laws which should be known and respected. The community's goals and objectives need to continually be brought to the consciousness of people, in a dynamic way, in order to stimulate the motivations and energies of each one. There needs to be a constant recourse to prayer, putting ourselves humbly before God. We all need to recognise the necessity of true and simple mutual dialogue, listening to each one, particularly to those in a minority or those members who are the poorest and the weakest. As a community we need to learn how to forgive and to celebrate while remaining simple and poor, because riches, like comfort, smother energies. The community must have recourse to the wisdom of experienced men and women from outside who can help evaluate the community. If we are not attentive to these things, we will gradually lose the inspiration that carries us forward. And if we lose that, we will begin to build barriers around ourselves and move towards division, separation, divorce and brokenness, towards the death of the community.

When a community becomes lukewarm and mediocre, its members suffer all kinds of frustrations. Relationships are no longer open and authentic. Energy to welcome, to love, and to celebrate is drained away; a sense of sterility dominates the group. When there is no longer an outlet for the emotions of each one, at a deep level, then aggression, sexual deviations and blockages appear.

Laws, rules and regulations cannot solve problems that arise. They tend only to aggravate things. They increase frustration, guilt and inner tensions, which must finally seek relief in some kind of compensation.

Permissiveness with regard to erotic sexuality, cut off from committed relationships, is the fruit of a culture without hope. The true solution lies, not in condemning this frenetic sexuality, but in the rediscovery of hope. In our times, the family community tends to be easily broken, with all the disastrous consequences this brings to the children, giving rise to anguished individualism, and frequently extreme fragility. It seems to me that we cannot recover health in human relationships, and the necessary energies to create communities which permit the integration of sexual drives, unless we turn to the Gospel message and the hope which it gives us. Ethics alone is not sufficient, because knowledge of a law does not give the necessary energy to abide by it.

It is especially difficult for those with a learning disability to find a harmony in their lives if they are not in a true community. They need relationships, intimacy, fecundity and celebration. It is not surprising that some turn to sexual relations, hoping against hope that they will find some fulfilment in them. But there is always disappointment following superficial relationships which do not lead to a true and permanent friendship, to a real covenant and sense of belonging one to another. Some, however, find a balance, albeit precarious, in the life of the couple where there is a friendship. I feel it is more just and more true to guide such couples towards marriage rather than leave them on a plateau of doubt concerning the permanence of their relationship. Instead of accepting too quickly that couples are made and unmade, it is better to call them either to be faithful to the relationship (and to give them the help they need for that) or to a dynamic community life. And of course, as a couple, they can be part of such a community.

I am moved by the pain of so many parents who are obliged to put their children in centres which encourage sexual activity as a liberation, and which lack a vision of faith and of what it means to be a human being that would give the unifying and inspirational force necessary for true community life. We have let parents manage as best they could alone. It is not surprising that parents coming from different philosophical and religious backgrounds have come together to create schools and residences, though, because of their very diversity, they have often not been able to create true communities, with the faith and inspiration that that implies.

Perhaps it is not too late to reverse the trend, if men and women of faith, open to the reality of community and conscious of the value of those with disabilities and their importance in society, work together to create or regenerate communities. Then perhaps there could be a rediscovery of the values of welcome and of love, right at the heart of society, where people with disabilities will be able to find their place and make their own contribution.

But, as long as there are no real communities, those with learning disabilities will find themselves at the bottom of the ladder of society, isolated, in anguish and in despair.

I am concerned about the future for people with such disabilities. Today, when everything is professionalised and considered from an economic viewpoint, the great risk is that they will be done away with before or right after birth, because they 'cost too much'. Efforts may be made to educate some people for 'normal' work or for work in sheltered workshops; but those with severe disabilities are in danger of being eliminated. Already, prenatal diagnosis, which in itself could be a good thing if there were remedies, leads frequently to abortion. And it is well known that more and more babies born with a disability are being killed at birth.

People with intellectual disabilities are an enigma for our society. Their very presence brings up many questions which are more or less unanswerable. It is difficult to see the meaning of their existence. Unable to develop their will and reason, their lives often appear fruitless and futile. In today's society, which is so organised and structured, they are seen as an economic burden. Their presence disturbs people.

Some people look at us in l'Arche as if we are completely mad, since we consider those whom society devalues as valuable, capable of awakening what is most precious in a human being – the heart, generosity, the dynamism of love. They incite us to put our intelligence at the service of love. They have a capacity to heal others by calling them to unify within themselves their deep emotions, their capacity for love and their reason. Thus, they can become sources of life.

A society which discards those who are weak and non-productive risks exaggerating the development of reason, organisa-tion, aggression and the desire to dominate. It becomes a society without a heart, without kindness – a rational and sad society, lack-ing celebration, divided within itself and given to competition, rivalry and, finally, violence.

The Gospel reveals to us the true meaning of the poor, the weak, and the non-productive. The message of Jesus is clear: the Good News is announced to the poor. That good news is that they will never be abandoned; they are loved by the Father who takes care of them. They *do* have a place; they *do* have value. Hidden in them is a mystery. In drawing near to them through the heart, we are drawn closer to God. They reveal what is most precious with-in us: our capacity to love and to be open others without judging them.

However, they can also reveal that which is hardest, most ego-tistical and most intolerant in us, precisely because they disturb and challenge us. They probe those places of fear, hate and anguish which are in each of us. Their cry for friendship reveals the fear that we have of friendship and, thus, they can stir up hate. The rich fear the poor, who disturb them! That is why they arrange things in such a way that they never see them or have contact with them. And then, they try to justify this rejection. The revelation of this presence of fear and hate in each of us can be salutary; it shows us the truth of our being, that truth which we do not like to acknowledge. None of us likes to have pointed out to us the powers of destruction and death within us. We want to appear good, strong and capable and to believe that we are the best, the elite. We do not want others to know that sometimes we are unjust, wrong and that darkness and fear are in us. Healing cannot take place, however, until our illusions have been exposed and our human reality and frailty acknowledged. It was only when I had touched my own fears and inner violence that I was able to let myself be touched more deeply by the presence of Jesus, gentle healer of hearts, the one who could liberate me from the powers of darkness within. Only then was I able to meet and touch the anguish and violence of others with deeper compassion. Only then was I able to truly understand the depth and the beauty of the gospel message.

The weak and the poor can heal the hearts of the strong and the rich and lead them to discover their own weakness and poverty – if they enter into a relationship with those who are weak and vulnerable. Those who are rich in the biblical sense of the word, have everything except the essential: the capacity to give and to give of themselves. Jesus said: 'How hard it is for those who have riches to enter the kingdom of God! It is easier for a camel to pass through the eye of a needle ...' The poor can help the rich to discover the value of love and sharing and thus lead them into the Kingdom of God.

Carl Jung once said how much he admired Christians because they saw Christ in the poor, in those who are hungry, naked, in hospital and in prison, and in those who are strangers.[1] What he could not understand was that they could not see Christ in their own poverty. We are all running away from the consciousness of our own weakness and vulnerability. We prefer to live in the illusions of our goodness. But in order to face the reality of our limits and our poverty, is it not essential that first of all we become aware that we are beloved by God *in* this very poverty?

I sense more and more, that only this acknowledgement of our own wounds, fragility and our poverty will enable us to live a true friendship with those who have a learning disability. Often we believe ourselves superior to them, their 'benefactors' and 'educators', we are unable to create community with them. The acknowledgement of our own limits and wounds allows us to draw nearer to their limits and wounds. Friendship begins with the acceptance of others as they are, without first wanting to change them. This is the friendship that persons with disabilities need most order to get out of the prison of loneliness and begin to live.

There is a danger for all us to want to climb the ladder of success, of power, and of possession. This encourages isolation, individualism; as we move upwards we can become more and more alone. Divisions are created between those who achieve success and those who do not. The latter then become discouraged and aggressive. Can we not reverse this urge to move upwards and encourage people to go down the ladder in order to meet those who are weaker, to create relationship with them? We will then create what everyone yearns for and needs the most: community. With the weakest at the heart of that community, we can celebrate our togetherness. But who has the authority, and above all, the necessary credibility to reverse the course of history? Is it not up to each one of us?

We all have to choose between two ways of being crazy: the foolishness of the Gospel or the non-sense of the values of our world. The Gospel is crazy: it sees in the weak and the poor a sign and a sacrament of God, thus revealing the mystery of Jesus and leading us to a true inner freedom, through a community life with celebrations and relationships. The values of the world are mad: they lead us to seek comfort and riches for ourselves, to reject others, to build protective walls around ourselves, and finally to arm ourselves for better defence. This leads finally to destruction. John Halsey, an Anglican priest of the Community of the Transfiguration in Scotland, once told a group from l'Arche: 'Either we will continue to *walk on* the poor and that will lead to the explosion of nuclear arms; or we will *walk with* the poor and that will lead to the transfiguration in Jesus Christ.'

Persons with learning disabilities will be able to live more humanly only if they find their place in authentic community life. That community life is rendered possible through the inspiration of the Gospel which sees those who are weakest as a positive source of inspiration and sees authority as service and not privilege.

Indeed, such a community life is necessary for all men and women on our earth. I doubt whether it is possible to resist the seductions of wealth and of power and all the superficial pleasures that are offered to distract us, if we do not share in a community of forgiveness and celebration, centred on the weak.

The more I experience my own humanity and reflect on the humanity of others whom I meet, the more I am aware of the depth of the wound within the heart of each one of us, whether it is husbands who hide or take refuge in work because they feel guilty and are no longer attracted to their wives, or wives who are bitter and wounded by lack of attention and love from their husbands, or parents in conflict with their children, or children stifled by parents who are too possessive. We are all wounded. We are wounded by sickness, wounded by a disability, wounded by the death of a dear one, wounded by the past, or by the non-acceptance of ourselves. Failures in work, and especially in relationships have left their wounds in us. Hate and fear, the experience of rejection (which makes us reject others) and of our inability to forgive, wound us. We have all been wounded by the blockages between people and groups, and by our own unfaithfulness and sin. Psychology may help unravel the origins of some of these wounds and help us to touch with less fear the pain and anguish within us. But it cannot heal the wounded heart, fill its emptiness, or wipe out the guilt of having wounded others.

We are in a society where these wounds continually fester. Fidelity is no longer valued and is sometimes even ridiculed. We are more preoccupied with the acquisition of riches or success, and above all avoidance of the pain and emptiness in our hearts by compensations and distractions which can never really satisfy. Family life today is in a serious crisis: more and more marriages fail, bringing a deep guilt in the heart of the man and the woman and deep pain for the children. These children will lack emotional maturity and stability; some can retain a deep insecurity or fear, leading sometimes to aggressive attitudes and real difficulties in the integration of their sexuality. Their anguish and their need to be loved can push them too quickly towards 'a love' without love.

So many men and women of our society are emotionally vulnerable and fragile because they lack the experience of being loved in a family or a community, a milieu which gives support, security, strength, peace and relaxation.

As authentic communities are born, hearts will slowly be healed, but the acquisition of maturity can take a long time, and a certain vulnerability can remain. This vulnerability is the lot of humanity. It comes from a dissonance between the desire in the heart of each one of us to be happy and the realities and disappointments of life. Each one of us experiences frustrations and dissatisfactions. Our hearts suffer from loneliness, feelings of failure and guilt; we all lack self confidence and can let ourselves be controlled by fear.

If however we live in a community, especially a community anchored in Jesus, we can find hope and strength to live the daily life, to struggle, despite all the forces of opposition, for a world of greater justice, compassion and love. We can find hope in the face of the anguish and the conflicts of our world: a hope which comes from the heart of God teaching us how to love, to understand, to forgive and to build peace.

L'Arche is still quite young. We are gradually discovering what we are called to be. We do not, of course, have the answers to the pain of all the members of our communities. Many have grown towards greater inner freedom, but there are others who still manifest a certain violence, moments of depression, sexual deviations and emotional blockages, some others can still be imprisoned in anger and psychoses. Isn't this the lot of so many other men and women in our world? Our role is to become their friends, to help them to carry their sufferings and to find a little light which will allow them to advance on the road of life. In trying to revive that tiny, fragile flame in the heart of the weak, l'Arche wants to become a little sign of hope in our anguished world.

The mystery of people with learning disabilities – and we could say the same thing for all those who are weak and put aside – is that they can become a source of life and truth, if we welcome them, enter into a relationship, a communion of hearts with them and put ourselves at their service.

When they feel welcomed and appreciated, many really find life and hope; they also give life and hope to others. In our world, with its divisions and hardness, people are often full of hate and strife. People with learning disabilities can teach men and women the road to trust, to love and to unity

This book is a witness to what we are experiencing and discovering in l'Arche, living close to men and women who have a learning disabilities. Their cry for relationship, for authentic love and for fruitfulness — far more profound than their desire for sexual pleasure — has revealed to us the deep cry for relationship, authentic love, and fruitfulness in every human being. We have so much to learn from those who, though stripped of power and knowledge, are so rich in their hearts and in their simplicity.

John Paul II spoke of this in January 2004 when he addressed the congress on the rights and dignity of people with disabilities:

> … disabled people are humanity's privileged witnesses. They can teach everyone about the love that saves us; they can become heralds of a new world, no longer dominated by force, violence and aggression, but by love, solidarity and acceptance, a new world transfigured by the light of Christ, the Son of God who became incarnate, who was crucified and rose for us.

Notes

2: Education and Its Demands

1. cf. John 10, where Jesus distinguishes the good shepherd from the hireling, who is hired for the job and is only interested in the salary.

3: The Relationship Between Man and Woman

1. From the Latin 'sponsus', spouse.
2. Pope John Paul II, General Audience of 20 February 1980, *L'Ossewatore Romano* (English edition), No. 8 (621), 25 February 1980.
3. Karl Stern, *Flight from Woman* (Allen & Unwin, 1966).
4. *Sexual Exploitation: What Parents of Handicapped People Should Know*, Seattle Rape Relief.
5. cf. chapter 2, pp. 28–9.
6. According to Martha Bala, MD, one out of three women in Canada has suffered sexual abuse and one out of four men.
7. She describes this in 'D'une réalité écrasante à une vraie vie: réflexions sur la prostitution', in the review *Femme et Monde*, Le Mouvement du Nid, National Secretariat, 7 rue de Landy, 92110 Clichy, France.

5: The Community: Place of Sexual Integration

1. Alain Giami, Chantal Humbert-Viveret and Dominique Laval, 'L'Ange et la Bête', *Les cahiers du CTNERHI*; Distributor PUF, Paris, 1983.
2. Ibid., pp. 71, 72.
3. 'Les besoins non couverts du jeune handicapé adult', *Les cahiers du CTNERHI*, no. 23, Paris.
4. The authors add that, if one wants to give a complete picture of the problems concerning sexuality and the affectivity of people with learning disabilities in institutions, one has to mention the way they are used frequently to gratify the needs of the staff. This exploitation finds two expressions:

- the traditional way, which is clandestine, brutal and violent, is rarely punished by institutional authorities and never publicised. It is more frequent than we are led to believe and is especially prevalent in the large 'traditional' institutions.

- the 'modern' way in more *avant-garde* institutions through the expression of a totally permissive ideology, and even under the pretext of 'healing through love'. The exercise of genital sexuality is practised in a quasi-open manner; it is vulgarised and accompanied not by violence, but by seduction which comes as much from the disabled person as from the staff. This seems less barbaric than the former way, but it is equally to be condemned. In fact, each time staff members, in the name of therapy, satisfy their own sexual needs they uses the disabled person as an object, and commits an 'institutional violence'.

5. See chapter 3, p. 66.
6. Message of John Paul II on the occasion of the International Symposium on the Dignity and Rights of the Mentally Disabled Person, January 2004.

6: Single People Living in Community

1. I use the word 'single' to emphasise a situation that is not really accepted. I use the word 'celibacy' as a situation accepted in a way of life with God and for God.

7: Unity in Marriage

1. John Paul II, *Familiaris Consortia: Regarding the Role of the Christian Family in the Modern World* (Catholic Truth Society S.357, 1981), p. 20.
2. 'Jaions pour l'accompagnement au mariage des personnes handicapées', thesis by Jacques Servais, presented at the University of Louvain la Neuve, 1981.
3. Ibid., p. 27.
4. Ibid., p. 113.
5. Robert B. Edgerton, *The Cloak of Competence* (University of California Press, 1967).

8: Fecundity and the Welcome of Death

1. In chapter 2 we have spoken of how difficult it is for the single parent to bring up a child.
2. December 2005. Copyright © 2005 Ateliers et Presses de Taizé, Taizé

Community, 71250 France.
3. cf. *Salvifici Doloris: The Apostolic Letter of John Paul II on Suffering*, 11 February 1984 (Catholic Truth Society, 1984).

9: A Celebration of Unity
1. General audience of 20 February 1980.

Conclusion
1. To Protestant pastors at Strasbourg, May 1932. *Collected Works*, vol. XI.